Issues

Annual Index
2008

Your one-stop reference guide to the ever-popular Issues series!

Complete A-Z index listings for all 64 Issues titles currently in print

A fully comprehensive research tool for your students

Now extended for even greater coverage!

First published by Independence
The Studio, High Green, Great Shelford
Cambridge CB22 5EG

ISBN 978 1 86168 463 9

Compiled by
Ann Shooter

Edited and typeset by
Lisa Firth

Printed in Great Britain
MWL Print Group Ltd

Cover
The illustration on the front cover is by
Don Hatcher.

A

A-levels (Advanced Level) **139**.4
  'dumbing down' claims **139**.19-20
  and gender **139**.10; **154**.22-3, 26
  results **139**.18
  science **139**.21
abortion
  access to abortions **126**.24
  after-effects **126**.10, 11, 14
  arguments against (pro-life) **126**.21-2, 25
  arguments for (pro-choice) **126**.21
  clinics **126**.12
  confidentiality **126**.13, 28, 29, 30
  costs **126**.12
  decision-making **126**.9-10, 12-13
    men **126**.15-16
    young people **126**.17-18
  definition **152**.2
  and depression **126**.11
  early medical abortion **126**.14, 33
  and emergency contraception (the morning after pill) **126**.24
  ethical considerations **126**.21-2
  and fetal abnormality **126**.9, 34, 35
  home abortions **126**.32-4
  and humanism **126**.4-5
  late abortion **126**.14, 37-8
  and the law **126**.5, 6, 7-8, 12
  and men **126**.15-16
  methods
    medical abortion ('the abortion pill') **126**.10, 14, 32-4
    vacuum aspiration ('the suction method') **126**.10, 14
  reasons for abortions **126**.8, 9, 21
    fetal abnormality **126**.9, 34, 35
    late abortions **126**.37
  religious positions on **126**.1-3, 6
  risks **126**.10, 14
    home abortions **126**.32, 34
  statistics **126**.18
  and teenage pregnancies **126**.29; **133**.2, 9
    under 16s **126**.13, 28, 29; **133**.2
  time limit **126**.12, 36-8
absenteeism **107**.6-8, 18
  from school, gender differences **154**.25
abuse
  as cause of self-harm **136**.1
  and young people **155**.19-26
abusers
  domestic, help for **155**.33-4
academic achievement *see* educational achievement
academic freedom **121**.8-9
academies **139**.14-16
access, disabled people **135**.3
access courses **139**.30
access rights, fathers **133**.39
accident warning devices, cars **119**.19
accidents
  alcohol-related **123**.16
  child labour and work-related **99**.1
  falls, older people **159**.4, 6
  road accidents, children **119**.5, 28, 30-31
acid rain **76**.11
acne **123**.28
active euthanasia **152**.5
active traffic management **119**.37-8

Volume numbers appear first (in bold) followed by page numbers; a change in volume number is preceded by a semi-colon.

Vol. **74** Money Matters
Vol. **76** The Water Crisis
Vol. **78** Threatened Species
Vol. **81** Alternative Therapies
Vol. **82** Protecting our Privacy
Vol. **85** The Housing Crisis
Vol. **88** Food and Nutrition
Vol. **89** Refugees
Vol. **96** Preventing Sexual Diseases
Vol. **97** Energy Matters
Vol. **99** Exploited Children
Vol. **100** Stress and Anxiety
Vol. **103** Animal Rights
Vol. **106** Trends in Marriage
Vol. **107** Work Issues
Vol. **115** Racial Discrimination
Vol. **116** Grief and Loss
Vol. **117** Self-Esteem and Body Image
Vol. **118** Focus on Sport
Vol. **119** Transport Trends
Vol. **120** The Human Rights Issue
Vol. **121** The Censorship Debate

Vol. **122** Bullying
Vol. **123** Young People and Health
Vol. **124** Parenting Issues
Vol. **125** Understanding Depression
Vol. **126** The Abortion Debate
Vol. **127** Eating Disorders
Vol. **128** The Cannabis Issue
Vol. **129** Gambling Trends
Vol. **130** Homelessness
Vol. **131** Citizenship and National Identity
Vol. **132** Child Abuse
Vol. **133** Teen Pregnancy and Lone Parents
Vol. **134** Customers and Consumerism
Vol. **135** Coping with Disability
Vol. **136** Self-Harm
Vol. **137** Crime and Anti-Social Behaviour
Vol. **138** A Genetically Modified Future?
Vol. **139** The Education Problem
Vol. **140** Vegetarian and Vegan Diets
Vol. **141** Mental Health
Vol. **142** Media Issues
Vol. **143** Problem Drinking

Vol. **144** The Cloning Debate
Vol. **145** Smoking Trends
Vol. **146** Sustainability and Environment
Vol. **147** The Terrorism Problem
Vol. **148** Religious Beliefs
Vol. **149** A Classless Society?
Vol. **150** Migration and Population
Vol. **151** Climate Change
Vol. **152** Euthanasia and the Right to Die
Vol. **153** Sexual Orientation and Society
Vol. **154** The Gender Gap
Vol. **155** Domestic Abuse
Vol. **156** Travel and Tourism
Vol. **157** The Problem of Globalisation
Vol. **158** The Internet Revolution
Vol. **159** An Ageing Population
Vol. **160** Poverty and Exclusion
Vol. **161** Waste Issues
Vol. **162** Staying Fit
Vol. **163** Drugs in the UK

Acts of Parliament **131**.24

acupressure **81**.1, 3

acupuncture **81**.5-6, 14, 23, 36

addictions **123**.8; **141**.9-10

    cannabis **128**.2, 8, 15

    gambling *see* compulsive gambling

    drugs **163**.2

    to the Internet **142**.37; **158**.38-9

    nicotine **123**.12; **145**.26

        children **145**.2-3

    online gaming **158**.39

    to self-harm **136**.9

    shopping **134**.13-14

    signs **123**.14

addictiveness of gambling **129**.30

ADHD (attention deficit and hyperactivity disorder) **141**.19

    and eating disorders **127**.10

adoption

    as alternative to abortion **126**.24

    by gay people **153**.31-2, 34

    and children's rights **120**.11

    and father's rights **133**.39

    process **133**.8-9

adult children

    parental interference **124**.14-15

    supported by parents **124**.3

advance directives (living wills) **152**.2, 35-6

    and the Mental Capacity Act **152**.37

advance fee scams **134**.26-7

advertising **134**.7-1

    anti-smoking **145**.18-19

    benefits of **134**.9

    and body image **117**.18

    and children **134**.10, 12

    cigarettes

        and children **145**.2

        EU ban **145**.7

    and drinking behaviour, young people **143**.17, 19, 20

    junk food **88**.10, 11, 19, 20, 35, 37

    online **158**.5

    radio **158**.6

    regulation **134**.7,10

    television **158**.5

adware **158**.34

affirmation and self-confidence **117**.34

affirmative action **154**.36

affluence *see* wealth

affordable housing **85**.29-31

    and the exception site policy **85**.28

    giving public money to private developers **85**.19

    Government strategies **130**.16, 33

    and housing associations **85**.19

    large houses **85**.11

    policies **85**.28-30

    and public sector workers **85**.1, 3, 4, 20, 21, 22

    in rural areas **85**.5, 28, 31

    shortage of **85**.1, 3, 8-9, 20; **130**.8, 23

    and social housing **85**.8

    and young workers **85**.3-4

age

    and alcohol consumption **123**.16-17; **143**.2, 17, 29

    and child labour **99**.2

    and child soldiers **99**.29-30

    of children and divorcing parents **106**.33-4; **124**.33-4

    and children's rights **120**.1,2

    of criminal responsibility **120**.12; **137**.11, 13

    of divorce **106**.3, 23, 25, 26

    and drinking behaviour, young people **143**.16

    and effects of alcohol **143**.7

    employment and gender **154**.29

    of first cohabitation **106**.10

    of first drink **143**.16, 21

    of first sexual intercourse **133**.1

    and first-time house buyers **85**.7

    of homeless people **130**.10, 14

    of immigrants **150**.8

    of lone parents **106**.3

    of marriage **106**.3, 25

    and sale of tobacco **145**.3

    of self-harmers **136**.4, 20

    of smokers **145**.1

    and social identity, by neighbourhood **149**.23

    and stress levels **100**.13

    and suicidal intent **136**.26

Volume numbers appear first (in bold) followed by page numbers; a change in volume number is preceded by a semi-colon.

Vol. **74** Money Matters

Vol. **76** The Water Crisis

Vol. **78** Threatened Species

Vol. **81** Alternative Therapies

Vol. **82** Protecting our Privacy

Vol. **85** The Housing Crisis

Vol. **88** Food and Nutrition

Vol. **89** Refugees

Vol. **96** Preventing Sexual Diseases

Vol. **97** Energy Matters

Vol. **99** Exploited Children

Vol. **100** Stress and Anxiety

Vol. **103** Animal Rights

Vol. **106** Trends in Marriage

Vol. **107** Work Issues

Vol. **115** Racial Discrimination

Vol. **116** Grief and Loss

Vol. **117** Self-Esteem and Body Image

Vol. **118** Focus on Sport

Vol. **119** Transport Trends

Vol. **120** The Human Rights Issue

Vol. **121** The Censorship Debate

Vol. **122** Bullying

Vol. **123** Young People and Health

Vol. **124** Parenting Issues

Vol. **125** Understanding Depression

Vol. **126** The Abortion Debate

Vol. **127** Eating Disorders

Vol. **128** The Cannabis Issue

Vol. **129** Gambling Trends

Vol. **130** Homelessness

Vol. **131** Citizenship and National Identity

Vol. **132** Child Abuse

Vol. **133** Teen Pregnancy and Lone Parents

Vol. **134** Customers and Consumerism

Vol. **135** Coping with Disability

Vol. **136** Self-Harm

Vol. **137** Crime and Anti-Social Behaviour

Vol. **138** A Genetically Modified Future?

Vol. **139** The Education Problem

Vol. **140** Vegetarian and Vegan Diets

Vol. **141** Mental Health

Vol. **142** Media Issues

Vol. **143** Problem Drinking

Vol. **144** The Cloning Debate

Vol. **145** Smoking Trends

Vol. **146** Sustainability and Environment

Vol. **147** The Terrorism Problem

Vol. **148** Religious Beliefs

Vol. **149** A Classless Society?

Vol. **150** Migration and Population

Vol. **151** Climate Change

Vol. **152** Euthanasia and the Right to Die

Vol. **153** Sexual Orientation and Society

Vol. **154** The Gender Gap

Vol. **155** Domestic Abuse

Vol. **156** Travel and Tourism

Vol. **157** The Problem of Globalisation

Vol. **158** The Internet Revolution

Vol. **159** An Ageing Population

Vol. **160** Poverty and Exclusion

Vol. **161** Waste Issues

Vol. **162** Staying Fit

Vol. **163** Drugs in the UK

victims of crime **137**.4
and voter turnout **131**.19
voting age lowering **120**.7-8; **131**.28, 29, 30
and worry about violent crime **137**.7
of young offenders **137**.14
age of consent **99**.25-6; **133**.1
age discrimination **159**.4, 8-13
young people **159**.12
age ratings
films **121**.23-5, 29-30
video games **121**.32-3
age-related macular degeneration **144**.22
ageing
ageing process **159**.1-2, 31-2
attitude to **159**.14-15
benefits of exercise **159**.33; **162**.12
and health **159**.31-9
effect of lifestyle **159**.33, 34
ageing population
global **150**.33, 35; **159**.5, 6
UK **150**.28, 29, 39; **159**.3
ageism *see* age discrimination
agriculture
and bioenergy **97**.18
and child labour **99**.1, 2, 4
coffee growers **157**.32, 33
cotton farming **157**.34
egg production **140**.38-9
exotic animals **140**.30
fairtrade *see* fair trade
and food nutrition **88**.31-4
and forests **146**.30
free trade in agriculture **88**.33
and global water shortages **76**.3, 4, 8
greenhouse gas production **151**.7
land use **146**.25
and migrant workers **150**.11
and new house-building **85**.28, 33
organic **146**.25
sustainable **146**.27
and water management **76**.18, 36
and water pollution **76**.11
agri-environment schemes **146**.25
agro-chemicals **138**.4
aid **160**.34-9
aid tying **157**.10
attitudes to **160**.35-6, 37
negative effects **160**.38-9
UK spending on aid **157**.9-10
AIDS (Acquired Immune Deficiency Syndrome) **96**.7, 17-22, 36-9
and assisted suicide **152**.31
and child labour **99**.3
and child soldiers **99**.31
deaths from **96**.36
and dementia **141**.7
and drug abuse **163**.11
education programmes **96**.32
global funding **96**.39
global statistics **96**.17-18, 24, 30, 36, 38
and medical research **103**.12, 13

older people as carers **159**.5
orphans **96**.39
pandemic **96**.31
and parents of lesbians and gay people **153**.9
and the sexual exploitation of children **99**.24
tackling stigma and discrimination **96**.19, 39
treatments **96**.18, 20
antiretroviral therapy (ART) **96**.36, 37, 38, 39
fixed dose combinations (FDCs) **96**.37
vaccines **96**.33-4
UK statistics **96**.20-2
and young people **96**.24-6, 29
air pollution **146**.35-6
monitoring **146**.37
and transport **119**.1, 15, 16, 31
air travel
airport security and congestion **156**.1
airport surveillance **120**.34
carbon dioxide emissions from **97**.25
and carbon offsetting **151**.22, 33, 39
disabled people **135**.9
effects of **156**.21
environmental impact **156**.21, 26
and pollution **119**.16
and privacy rights **82**.3
security **147**.32
and UK travel trends **156**.3; **161**.32
al-Qaida **147**.7
alcohol **88**.7, 24; **123**.14-19
and accidents **123**.16
advertising, effects on young people **143**.17, 19, 20
alcopops **143**.1, 3
beer **143**.1
and brain function
calories in **143**.2
consumption
children **143**.20
older people **143**.9-10, 30
regional variations **143**.13
worldwide increase **143**.5
young people **123**.1-2, 9, 18-19; **143**.2, 5, 15, 20, 37
daily benchmarks **143**.8, 25, 26-7, 34
awareness of **143**.11, 34
deaths related to **143**.3, 6, 37; **163**.11
and depression **125**.2, 3, 36-7
and domestic violence **155**.4
drinks industry and responsible drinking **143**.27
and drugs **143**.3, 10
effects of **123**.15-16, 18; **125**.37; **143**.3, 7, 23
health benefits of **143**.4, 7, 27
health risks of **143**.6, 9-10
and the law **143**.2-3
young people **143**.2, 17
licences **143**.2
and life expectancy **143**.13
and mental health **141**.34
and pregnancy **143**.3, 25, 27, 33-4
purchasing **143**.11
underage **143**.16, 17, 20, 28
responsible drinking **143**.26-7, 29
risks

of alcohol consumption **143**.3, 21-2
of binge drinking **143**.4, 15
in pregnancy **143**.3, 33
as self-medication for mental health problems **125**.36-7
spirits **143**.1
strength **123**.16; **143**.1, 10
and stress **100**.27, 31, 37, 39
support groups **123**.17; **143**.38, 39
and television **143**.18-19, 20
trends **143**.1-24
UK legislation on the sale of **143**.2
underage drinking **125**.9; **137**.14; **143**.16, 20, 28
units of **143**.1, 26
awareness of **143**.11
drink labelling **143**.30, 32
and violence **137**.8
wine
health benefits **143**.4
strength **143**.1
alcohol abuse **143**.25-39
costs of **143**.36
government strategies **143**.36-7
and homeless people **130**.11, 12, 20
and older people **143**.9-10, 30
risks **143**.3, 4, 9, 13, 14
signs of **143**.25, 35
statistics **143**.37
street drinking **130**.12
treatment **143**.35, 38-9
young people **143**.29, 37
alcolocks **119**.8-9
alcopops **143**.1, 3
algae biofuels **151**.24-5
allergens, definition of **138**.4
alternative burials **116**.36, 38
alternative tourism **156**.24
aluminium recycling **161**.22, 27
Alzheimer's disease **141**.6; **159**.4, 36-9
and animal experimentation **144**.34
diagnosis using eye test **141**.19
and diet **125**.12
amino acids **140**.7, 23

amnesia **141**.11
amphetamines **163**.4-5, 25
amphibians
and evolution **78**.1
and the exotic pet trade **78**.21
anabolic agents/steroids
and the law **118**.35, 36
anaesthesia, and animal experiments **103**.6, 8, 9, 12, 22
anger
and bereavement **116**.4, 8, 19
dealing with **136**.3
and domestic violence **155**.4, 34
and sexual abuse, dealing with **132**.28
and traumatic bereavement **116**.11
anger management
for bullies **122**.18
and domestic abuse **155**.34
Anglicanism *see* Church of England
angling **103**.30
and mental well-being **117**.38
animal cloning **144**.30-39
Dolly the sheep **144**.1, 15, 30-31, 32, 34, 39
and factory farming **144**.35
and food production **144**.36-9
and milk production **144**.36-8, 39
risks **144**.39
animal cruelty **103**.32-9
and abuse **103**.32
and animal welfare law **103**.33-5
education in preventing **103**.35
and the fur trade **103**.36-9
statistics **103**.34-5
animal experiments **103**.1-23
alternatives to **103**.7, 9, 10, 13-14, 17-19, 22, 23
clinical studies **103**.7, 18, 22
computer research **103**.13-14, 17, 19, 22
epidemiology (population studies) **103**.17, 18, 19, 22
reasons for not using **103**.19
reasons for using **103**.19
tissue and cell cultures **103**.14, 17-18, 19, 22
and animal rights activists **103**.2, 9
and the anti-vivisection belief system **103**.22-3

Volume numbers appear first (in bold) followed by page numbers; a change in volume number is preceded by a semi-colon.

Vol. **74** Money Matters
Vol. **76** The Water Crisis
Vol. **78** Threatened Species
Vol. **81** Alternative Therapies
Vol. **82** Protecting our Privacy
Vol. **85** The Housing Crisis
Vol. **88** Food and Nutrition
Vol. **89** Refugees
Vol. **96** Preventing Sexual Diseases
Vol. **97** Energy Matters
Vol. **99** Exploited Children
Vol. **100** Stress and Anxiety
Vol. **103** Animal Rights
Vol. **106** Trends in Marriage
Vol. **107** Work Issues
Vol. **115** Racial Discrimination
Vol. **116** Grief and Loss
Vol. **117** Self-Esteem and Body Image
Vol. **118** Focus on Sport
Vol. **119** Transport Trends
Vol. **120** The Human Rights Issue
Vol. **121** The Censorship Debate

Vol. **122** Bullying
Vol. **123** Young People and Health
Vol. **124** Parenting Issues
Vol. **125** Understanding Depression
Vol. **126** The Abortion Debate
Vol. **127** Eating Disorders
Vol. **128** The Cannabis Issue
Vol. **129** Gambling Trends
Vol. **130** Homelessness
Vol. **131** Citizenship and National Identity
Vol. **132** Child Abuse
Vol. **133** Teen Pregnancy and Lone Parents
Vol. **134** Customers and Consumerism
Vol. **135** Coping with Disability
Vol. **136** Self-Harm
Vol. **137** Crime and Anti-Social Behaviour
Vol. **138** A Genetically Modified Future?
Vol. **139** The Education Problem
Vol. **140** Vegetarian and Vegan Diets
Vol. **141** Mental Health
Vol. **142** Media Issues
Vol. **143** Problem Drinking

Vol. **144** The Cloning Debate
Vol. **145** Smoking Trends
Vol. **146** Sustainability and Environment
Vol. **147** The Terrorism Problem
Vol. **148** Religious Beliefs
Vol. **149** A Classless Society?
Vol. **150** Migration and Population
Vol. **151** Climate Change
Vol. **152** Euthanasia and the Right to Die
Vol. **153** Sexual Orientation and Society
Vol. **154** The Gender Gap
Vol. **155** Domestic Abuse
Vol. **156** Travel and Tourism
Vol. **157** The Problem of Globalisation
Vol. **158** The Internet Revolution
Vol. **159** An Ageing Population
Vol. **160** Poverty and Exclusion
Vol. **161** Waste Issues
Vol. **162** Staying Fit
Vol. **163** Drugs in the UK

arguments against **103**.2, 5-7; **144**.34
arguments for **103**.2, 9
benefits of in scientific research **103**.3
cosmetic testing **103**.23
and cruelty **103**.6-7, 9, 22
and fears of endangering patients **103**.21
and genetic research **103**.11
and genetically modified animals **103**.1, 8; **144**.34
and humanism **140**.32-3
and the law **103**.16, 20
and medical advances **103**.10-11
and moral justification **103**.7
public attitudes to **147**.20
questions and answers on **103**.10-11
regulation of **103**.1-2, 16, 20, 21
replacement of **103**.9
statistics **103**.1, 4, 8
and toxicological procedures **103**.8, 10
types of animals used in **103**.1, 5-6, 8, 22
unreliability of **103**.6
and veterinary research **103**.10
animal fat as food ingredient **140**.18
animal feed **88**.35-6
GM content **138**.25, 26
animal-human embryos **144**.9, 11, 13, 14, 20
animal rights **103**.32-3
animal rights activists
and animal experiments **103**.2, 9, 11
Government policies on **103**.23
laws against **103**.15-16
terrorism **147**.20-25
animal sentience **140**.27-8
animal suffering **140**.32
animal welfare **88**.32-3, 35-6; **140**.27-39
consumer attitudes **140**.14, 31, 33
egg production **140**.38-9
Freedom Food mark **140**.34
And humanism **140**.31-3
meat production **140**.13
organic farms **140**.35-6
UK legislation on **121**.7
anorexia nervosa **123**.7, 33-4; **127**.1, 11-12
as auto-immune disease **127**.12
children and young people **127**.20
anti-bullying practices
schools **122**.18, 25
workplaces **122**.39
anti-consumerism **146**.39
anti-depressant drugs **125**.24-5, 32
and adolescents **125**.8, 27
and children **123**.28; **125**.27
and postnatal depression **125**.18
and seasonal affective disorder **125**.38
and young people **123**.28
anti-doping initiatives **118**.25-8
international **118**.27-8, 31-2
UK **118**. 26-7, 28, 30
anti-psychotic drugs **125**.19
anti-racism
and football **118**.14
laws *see* legislation and racism

anti-social behaviour
adults unwilling to intervene **137**.26, 27
and homelessness **130**.7
impact of interventions **137**.35
by young people **137**.17
young people's concerns about **137**.24
Anti-Social Behaviour Orders (ASBOs) **137**.4, 12, 21-3, 35
anti-social driving habits **119**.9
anti-terrorism measures
and deportation **120**.38-9
and identity cards **120**.35
legislation **147**.2, 3, 27, 35-6
Muslims' views on **115**.34
antibiotics **88**.14
and medical research **103**.12
and organic farming **140**.35
resistance to **138**.4
and genetically modified organisms **138**.13
antiretroviral therapy (ART) **96**.36, 37, 38, 39
anxiety
and childhood depression **125**.28
dangers of severe **100**.21
defining **100**.21
and depression **100**.24
and stress **100**.2, 21
symptoms of **100**.21
appearance, effects of smoking **145**.30-31
appetite-suppressing hormones **127**.38-9
apprenticeships **107**.36
aquaculture (fish farming) **146**.29
aquifers, and global water supplies **76**.7, 16, 19
armed conflict
and the sexual exploitation of children **99**.20-1
war-affected children **99**.32-3
armed forces
homeless ex-servicemen **130**.11
recruitment age **120**.20
suicide of soldiers, Japan **136**.39
aromatherapy **81**.23, 36
and cancer **81**.10, 33
and multiple sclerosis **81**.30
questions and answers **81**.10
and scientists **81**.28, 29
and stress relief **100**.37
arranged marriages **106**.15-18
arrests
for drug use **128**.11
your rights **128**.35-6
of young offenders **137**.7
arts therapies **141**.38
AS-levels (Advanced Supplementary levels) **139**.4, 18
asbestos disposal **161**.23
ASBOs (Anti-Social Behaviour Orders) **137**.4, 12, 21-3, 35
Asian people
Asian-British women and body image **117**.29
British identity **115**.37
footballers **118**.13, 15-16
Asperger's syndrome **135**.34
aspirations gap **107**.2
assault on children **120**.14-15
in detention centres **120**.17

assertiveness training **117**.3
  and stress **100**.32
Assisted Dying bill **152**.16, 17, 33
  and disability rights **135**.24
assisted suicide **152**.1, 3, 5, 8-9
  arguments against **152**.20-21
  arguments for **152**.20
  and disabled people **135**.24; 20-21
  and palliative care **152**.22
  physician-assisted suicide **152**.5, 7-8, 29-30, 31
asthma
  increasing **119**.13, 26, 31
  and passive smoking **145**.28, 29
asylum seekers **120**.31; **150**.23
  in Britain *see* Britain, asylum seekers
  children **120**.21-2
  conditions for granting refugee status **89**.1
  fleeing from conflict **89**.7-8
  and HIV **96**.39
    and homelessness **130**.11-12, 19
  and housing **85**.2, 13
  illegal immigration and identity cards **82**.2, 7, 8, 9, 10, 11
  numbers of **89**.2, 5, 6, 10
  top asylum nationalities **89**.1-2, 5, 6, 10
  top countries receiving **89**.2, 5, 10
athletics and drugs *see* drugs in sport
attempted suicide **136**.27-8
  and gender **136**.33
  and stress in young people **100**.4
attention deficit disorder (ADD) **127**.7
  and eating disorders **127**.10
attention deficit and hyperactivity disorder (ADHD) **141**.19
  and eating disorders **127**.10
attention-seeking and self-harm **136**.2-3, 8
authoritarian parenting style **124**.8; **132**.18
authoritative parenting style **124**.8; **132**.18
autism **135**.34
auto-immune disease, anorexia as **127**.12
autonomy **152**.6
  effect of legalising euthanasia **152**.6
  loss of, disabled people **152**.20
  and right to die **152**.3

aviation security **147**.32

B

babies
  and euthanasia debate **152**.4, 32, 33, 34
  and HIV **96**.31, 39
  and mother's smoking **145**.32-3
bacteria **88**.27, 28-9
  transgenic **144**.11
baculoviruses **138**.13-14
banks
  basic bank accounts **74**.18, 24
  children and bank accounts **74**.6-7, 13
  current accounts **74**.18-19, 24
  financial education programmes for schools **74**.13
  Internet banking **74**.2
  and money management **106**.14
  overdrafts **74**.1, 18, 19, 21-2, 37
  savings accounts **74**.13, 19, 24
  and students **74**.2, 17, 21-2
  and young people **74**.9, 17-19
bariatric (weight loss) surgery **162**.3, 20
batteries, recycling **161**.23, 28
battery eggs
  supermarket bans **140**.38
BBC
  funding **142**.6
  and portrayal of homosexuality **153**.24
beer
  strength **143**.1
  and young people **123**.1
begging **130**.12
  children as beggars **99**.3, 4
  giving to beggars **130**.32
behaviour
  effects of cannabis use **128**.16
  effects of child abuse **132**.23
  children, effect of poverty **160**.13
  gender differences **154**.1, 9
  and healthy self-esteem **117**.30

Volume numbers appear first (in bold) followed by page numbers; a change in volume number is preceded by a semi-colon.

Vol. **74** Money Matters
Vol. **76** The Water Crisis
Vol. **78** Threatened Species
Vol. **81** Alternative Therapies
Vol. **82** Protecting our Privacy
Vol. **85** The Housing Crisis
Vol. **88** Food and Nutrition
Vol. **89** Refugees
Vol. **96** Preventing Sexual Diseases
Vol. **97** Energy Matters
Vol. **99** Exploited Children
Vol. **100** Stress and Anxiety
Vol. **103** Animal Rights
Vol. **106** Trends in Marriage
Vol. **107** Work Issues
Vol. **115** Racial Discrimination
Vol. **116** Grief and Loss
Vol. **117** Self-Esteem and Body Image
Vol. **118** Focus on Sport
Vol. **119** Transport Trends
Vol. **120** The Human Rights Issue
Vol. **121** The Censorship Debate

Vol. **122** Bullying
Vol. **123** Young People and Health
Vol. **124** Parenting Issues
Vol. **125** Understanding Depression
Vol. **126** The Abortion Debate
Vol. **127** Eating Disorders
Vol. **128** The Cannabis Issue
Vol. **129** Gambling Trends
Vol. **130** Homelessness
Vol. **131** Citizenship and National Identity
Vol. **132** Child Abuse
Vol. **133** Teen Pregnancy and Lone Parents
Vol. **134** Customers and Consumerism
Vol. **135** Coping with Disability
Vol. **136** Self-Harm
Vol. **137** Crime and Anti-Social Behaviour
Vol. **138** A Genetically Modified Future?
Vol. **139** The Education Problem
Vol. **140** Vegetarian and Vegan Diets
Vol. **141** Mental Health
Vol. **142** Media Issues
Vol. **143** Problem Drinking

Vol. **144** The Cloning Debate
Vol. **145** Smoking Trends
Vol. **146** Sustainability and Environment
Vol. **147** The Terrorism Problem
Vol. **148** Religious Beliefs
Vol. **149** A Classless Society?
Vol. **150** Migration and Population
Vol. **151** Climate Change
Vol. **152** Euthanasia and the Right to Die
Vol. **153** Sexual Orientation and Society
Vol. **154** The Gender Gap
Vol. **155** Domestic Abuse
Vol. **156** Travel and Tourism
Vol. **157** The Problem of Globalisation
Vol. **158** The Internet Revolution
Vol. **159** An Ageing Population
Vol. **160** Poverty and Exclusion
Vol. **161** Waste Issues
Vol. **162** Staying Fit
Vol. **163** Drugs in the UK

and low self-esteem **117**.5
    problems in schools **120**.16
    stress and behavioural changes **100**.33
    symptoms of workplace bullying **122**.31
benefits *see* state benefits
benzene emissions **119**.15; **146**.36
bereavement **116**.1-18
    children *see* children and bereavement
    counselling **116**.6
    feelings **116**.1, 3-4, 5, 7-9, 10-11, 19, 21-2, 30
    help from GP **116**.2
    by murder **116**.8
    and stress in young people **100**.2
    by suicide **116**.8
    support **116**.2, 14-15
betting **129**.2
bias and the media **142**.10
Big Issue, The **130**.33, 37
bill payments
    and direct debit **74**.9, 23
    and young people **74**.2, 23
Bills (parliamentary) **131**.24
binge buying **134**.13, 14
binge drinking **143**.4, 13, 14
    children **143**.20
    Europe **143**.31
    older people **143**.9-10, 30
    parents' worries about **124**.17
    risks **143**.4, 14
    young people **143**.5, 15
binge eating **127**.2, 15-16
bingo **129**.2
biodegradability of litter **161**.16
biodiesel vehicles **119**.21
biodiversity **146**.18-21, 33
    and climate change **151**.9
    and endangered animals **78**.6
    framework for measuring **78**.27
    loss of freshwater **76**.35
    protecting **146**.20-21
    Scotland **146**.21
    threats to **146**.19, 21
    value of **146**.18-19
biodynamic massage **81**.1
bioenergy **97**.18
    biofuels **97**.9; **138**.4; **146**.39; **151**.24-5
    biomass **97**.5, 6, 9, 11, 18
biological attacks, response to **147**.31
biological parents and parental responsibility **153**.33
biology
    and gender development **154**.1
    and sexual orientation **153**.6, 7
biometrics **120**.33-4
biotechnology
    definition **138**.4
    public attitudes to **138**.15-16; **144**.19
bipolar affective disorder (manic depression) **125**.2, 4, 10,
       19-20; **141**.14-15
    defining **125**.19
    experiences of sufferers **141**.28-9
    symptoms **125**.19

    treatments **125**.19-20
birth control, teenagers **123**.22-3
    awareness of birth control services **123**.3
birth rates
    births outside marriage **106**.4; **124**.22
    fall in **106**.2
    to foreign parents in UK **150**.29, 30
    to teenage mothers **133**.2
bisexuality **153**.10-12
    definition **153**.1
    discrimination **153**.2
blame, feelings of
    following bereavement **116**.8, 11, 19
    and low self-esteem **117**.6
blasphemy laws **121**.16
    and cartoons of Mohammed **121**.12
blended families **124**.39
blogs **142**.37; **158**.3, 8
blood doping **118**.38
blood pressure *see* high blood pressure (hypertension)
blood products, and HIV **96**.14
blood sugar levels **88**.15
    and binge eating **127**.15
blood tests for diagnosing mental illness **141**.18
blue badge scheme (disabled people) **135**.7-8
BMI *see* body mass index
body dysmorphic disorder/dysmorphophobia **127**.18-19
body image **117**.10-30
    assessment of **117**.18
    boys **117**.23
    and eating disorders **127**.27
    and ethnicity **117**.29-30
    and exercise **141**.39
    girls **117**.19, 20-21, 22, 25
    improving **117**.10-11, 15, 18-19
    and the media **117**.11-12, 15, 17-18; **127**.23, 25-6, 27
    negative
        girls **117**.25
        teenage girls **117**.20-22
        women **117**.14-15
    positive **117**.10
    and self-esteem **117**.10-11
    study **127**.29
    women **117**.19
        and ethnicity **117**.29-30
        and media pressure **117**.11-12, 14-15
        timeline **117**.16-17
body mass index (BMI) **88**.8; **127**.32; **162**.1, 4, 23
    and children **127**.36; **162**.1
    criticism of **162**.5
body weight **88**.1, 12, 18
    and smoking **145**.30-31
bonded labour **120**.29
bone density, effects of eating disorders **127**.5
bone marrow stem cells
    and heart disease treatment **144**.23
    and sperm cell creation **144**.29
bone marrow transplants **144**.24
border controls **89**.20; **147**.29
boys and young men
    and body image **117**.23

and child labour 99.2

child soldiers 99.31, 36

and eating disorders 123.33

and education 154.22-6

    foundation stage 154.23

    raising educational achievement 154.25

    single-sex teaching 154.26

    subject choices 154.22, 26

    underachievement 154.23

and mental health problems 141.1

and parenthood 133.25-7

and puberty 127.22

self-harm 136.7

sexual exploitation of 99.16, 21

and smoking 145.2, 5

street children 99.19

brain

    effects of alcohol on 125.37; 143.4

    effects of cannabis on 128.34

    effect of diet 141.30-31

    effect of nicotine 145.25, 26

    stem cell therapy for brain damage 144.22

brand awareness, children 134.11

brand image and advertising 134.8-9

brand names as children's names 134.12

breast cancer and complementary therapies 81.23

breast surgery, teenagers 117.26-8

Bretton Woods 157.5

Britain, asylum seekers

    appeals process 89.13-14, 29, 33

    asylum claims procedure 89.12, 13-14

    asylum legislation 89.11, 12, 33, 39

    citizenship acceptance 89.37

    costs of the asylum system 89.11, 30

    detention centres 89.12, 13

    health treatment 89.19-20

    legal aid 89.29

    number of asylum claims 89.16, 18, 23; 150.4, 23

    refused asylum applications 89.11, 13-14, 18

    welfare support 89.12, 13, 14, 19, 30, 38

British history, importance of teaching 131.7

British identity 131.1-14; 156.11

Asians 115.37

    and non-white ethnic groups 115.38

British mentality and class 149.6

British population

    ethnic groups 115.3

    mixed-race relationships 115.24

British tourists

    behaviour 156.31

    visits abroad 156.4

Britishness 131.1-14

    decline of 131.9

    effect of devolution 131.5, 6

    and Islamophobia 131.11

    and multiculturalism 131.10

broadband services 158.5-6, 17

    for low-income families 158.18

broadcasting

    illegal 142.7

    mergers 142.4

Broadcasting Code 121.36

broadcasting regulation 121.36-7

broadsheet newspapers 142.8

brownfield sites

    and agricultural land 85.28

    decontaminating 85.22

    and new house-building 85.9, 26, 34

    and wildlife in London 85.16-17

Buddhism 148.2

    abortion and contraception 126.3

    festivals 148.2

    food rules 148.11

budgeting

    and students 74.2, 28, 30, 32

    and young people 74.2, 3, 14-15, 23

building industry see construction industry

building waste recycling 161.23

bulimia nervosa 123.7; 127.1-2, 13-14

    children and young people 127.20

bullies

    anger management training 122.18

    how to stop bullying 122.2, 9-10

    no-blame policy 122.6-7

Volume numbers appear first (in bold) followed by page numbers; a change in volume number is preceded by a semi-colon.

Vol. 74 Money Matters

Vol. 76 The Water Crisis

Vol. 78 Threatened Species

Vol. 81 Alternative Therapies

Vol. 82 Protecting our Privacy

Vol. 85 The Housing Crisis

Vol. 88 Food and Nutrition

Vol. 89 Refugees

Vol. 96 Preventing Sexual Diseases

Vol. 97 Energy Matters

Vol. 99 Exploited Children

Vol. 100 Stress and Anxiety

Vol. 103 Animal Rights

Vol. 106 Trends in Marriage

Vol. 107 Work Issues

Vol. 115 Racial Discrimination

Vol. 116 Grief and Loss

Vol. 117 Self-Esteem and Body Image

Vol. 118 Focus on Sport

Vol. 119 Transport Trends

Vol. 120 The Human Rights Issue

Vol. 121 The Censorship Debate

Vol. 122 Bullying

Vol. 123 Young People and Health

Vol. 124 Parenting Issues

Vol. 125 Understanding Depression

Vol. 126 The Abortion Debate

Vol. 127 Eating Disorders

Vol. 128 The Cannabis Issue

Vol. 129 Gambling Trends

Vol. 130 Homelessness

Vol. 131 Citizenship and National Identity

Vol. 132 Child Abuse

Vol. 133 Teen Pregnancy and Lone Parents

Vol. 134 Customers and Consumerism

Vol. 135 Coping with Disability

Vol. 136 Self-Harm

Vol. 137 Crime and Anti-Social Behaviour

Vol. 138 A Genetically Modified Future?

Vol. 139 The Education Problem

Vol. 140 Vegetarian and Vegan Diets

Vol. 141 Mental Health

Vol. 142 Media Issues

Vol. 143 Problem Drinking

Vol. 144 The Cloning Debate

Vol. 145 Smoking Trends

Vol. 146 Sustainability and Environment

Vol. 147 The Terrorism Problem

Vol. 148 Religious Beliefs

Vol. 149 A Classless Society?

Vol. 150 Migration and Population

Vol. 151 Climate Change

Vol. 152 Euthanasia and the Right to Die

Vol. 153 Sexual Orientation and Society

Vol. 154 The Gender Gap

Vol. 155 Domestic Abuse

Vol. 156 Travel and Tourism

Vol. 157 The Problem of Globalisation

Vol. 158 The Internet Revolution

Vol. 159 An Ageing Population

Vol. 160 Poverty and Exclusion

Vol. 161 Waste Issues

Vol. 162 Staying Fit

Vol. 163 Drugs in the UK

reasons for bullying 122.8-9
bullying 122.1-39
   bullying behaviour 122.8, 9-10, 15-16
   cyber-bullying 122.19-26
   definition 122.1, 5, 8
   extent of 122.11, 17, 22-3
   fears of gay parents 153.22
   gender differences 154.25
   homophobic 153.14-18
   reasons for 122.8-9
   responding to bullying 122.1-2, 5-6, 13, 16; 123.3
      cyber-bullying 122.19, 20, 21, 23, 24
      workplace bullying 122.27, 31-2, 33, 37-8
   and stress in young people 100.1, 2, 4
   types of bullying 122.15-116, 18
   at work 122.27-39
   and workplace stress 100.14, 15
   and young people 122.1-18
burial 116.37-9
   alternative burials 116.36, 38
   natural 134.31
   on private land 116.39
   at sea 116.39
bus travel
   and disabled people 135.8-9
   and pollution 119.12
   trends 119.1
businesses
   anti-terrorism measures 147.32
   and biodiversity protection 146.20
   and environmentalism 146.38-9
   sustainable 146.7

C

caffeine 118.35
   and mental health 141.35
calcium 88.6
   dietary sources 140.4
   teenagers' requirements 123.6-7
   and vegetarian diets 140.3
calorie content of alcohol 143.2
calorie intake 88.1, 12; 162.8
camera phones and bullying 122.22-3, 26
campaigns
   joining, and raising self-esteem 117.33
   and the media 142.10
cancer
   and cannabis use 128.17, 19, 28
   and complementary therapies 81.3, 10, 21, 27, 32-3
   leukaemia, stem cell therapy 144.21
   lung cancer 145.34
   and passive smoking 145.2, 29
   prevention 88.17, 30
   research and animal experiments 103.8, 10, 13
   and smoking 145.34
   stem cell therapy for blood cancers 144.21
   and vegetarian diets 140.9, 11
cancer salves (escharotics) 81.33
cancer treatments

and genetically modified hens 138.20-21
cannabinoids 118.38
   and multiple sclerosis 128.36
   THC 128.3, 34
cannabis 163.6
   appearance 128.1
   cannabis cafés 27-8
   cannabis oil 128.4, 6, 23
   cannabis resin (hashish) 128.1, 3, 6, 23
      seizures of 128.31
   chemical content 128.13-14
   children's use 128.16
      and depression 128.14
   classification 128.13
   compulsive use 128.15
   cultivation 128.23-4; 33-4; 163.25
      penalties for 128.31
      skunk 128.3-4
   dealing, penalties for 128.2, 9, 13
   dependence on 128.2, 8, 15
   and driving 128.14
   eating 128.5
   effects of 163.6, 35-6
      desired 128.4, 14
      harmful 128.1-2, 4-5, 8-9, 13-15, 28
      on the brain 128.34
      on learning and educational performance 128.14
      medicinal 128.4, 28, 36, 37
      skunk 128.2
   forms of 128.1, 3-4, 6, 13
   giving up 128.2, 10
   and hard drug use 128.9-10, 11, 28
   herbal cannabis (marijuana/grass) 128.2,3,6, 23
      seizures of 128.31
   history 128.7
   home cultivation of 128.3-4, 30-31
   and the law 128.2, 7, 9, 26-38
   legalisation debate 128.7
   market 128.23-4
   medicinal use of 128.4, 28, 36, 37
      and the law 128.37
      and multiple sclerosis 81.30, 31; 128.36, 37
   and mental health 128.5, 8, 14-15; 163.35
   and multiple sclerosis 81.30, 31; 128.36, 37
   names for 128.1
   penalties
      for cultivation 128.31
      for possession 128.2, 9, 13, 27, 30, 31, 32
      for supply 128.2, 9, 13
   potency of 128.6
      resin 128.3
      skunk 128.2
   prices 128.2, 6
   production see cannabis cultivation
   psychosis 128.15
   purity 128.1, 2
   reclassification of 128.13, 26-8, 29; 163.32, 35-6
      criticized 128.38
      effect on health 128.30-32, 38
      public attitudes to 128.12
   and respiratory health 128.18-19

seizures of **128**.23, 31

smoking **128**.8

  effects of **128**.5, 18-19

sources **128**.3, 34

THC (delta-9 tetrahydrocannabinol) **128**.3, 34

use

  Britain **163**.7

  Europe **128**.21-2; **163**.25

  giving up **128**.2, 10

  methods of use **128**.5, 6, 13

  prevalence **128**.6, 21, 22

  public attitudes to **128**.12

users, children **128**.16

carbohydrates **88**.2, 5-6, 15

carbon

  carbon credits **151**.36-7

  low carbon technologies **97**.4

carbon dioxide

  atmospheric concentration **151**.7

  CO_2 equivalent **151**.13

  sources of **151**.4

carbon dioxide emissions

  agriculture **151**.7

  and air transport **97**.25

  and biomass **97**.18

  from fossil fuel burning **97**.1, 4

  from power stations **97**.3

  and global warming **151**.3

  public awareness of **97**.34

  reducing **97**.2; **151**.2, 13

  from tourism **156**.25

  from transport **119**.14, 15, 16, 24, 30

  in the UK **97**.5, 21

carbon monoxide **146**.36

  transport emissions **119**.15

carbon offsetting **151**.20-22, 33-5; **156**.1

carbon sequestration **151**.26

carbon sinks **151**.26

carbon trading **151**.36-7

cardboard recycling **161**.24, 26-7

cardiology, stem cell therapy **144**.22, 23, 28

cardiovascular disease *see* heart disease

care gap **135**.20

care homes **159**.27-8

care leavers and homelessness **130**.11, 14

care services for older people **159**.4

  concerns about **159**.28

  funding **159**.29

  rising costs **159**.26

career advice **107**.32

  gender bias **154**.28, 35

career breaks **107**.27

career progression **107**.28

carers

  and flexible working **107**.17-18

  older people as carers **159**.4, 5

  statistics **154**.30

  young carers **135**.10-12

carrier bags *see* plastic bags

cars

  attitudes to car use **97**.35, 36

  batteries, recycling **161**.28

  car clubs **119**.33

  cleaner fuels **119**.20-23

  congestion *see* congestion, traffic

  dependency on **119**.7

  drink-driving *see* drink-driving

  emissions reduction **151**.39

  fuel efficient **119**.20-24

  ownership **119**.7, 11, 29

  recycling **161**.23

  reducing use of **119**.39

  sharing **119**.32-3

  speeding **119**.3, 4, 8

    and pedestrian injuries **119**.5, 30-31

    and speed cameras **119**.4, 17, 18

    speed limiters **119**.18

  spending on **134**.4, 25

  tax and fuel efficiency **119**.24

  usage trends **119**.1, 7-9, 11, 13, 29; **161**.31

cartoons of Mohammed **121**.10-13, 15-16; **142**.34

cashless society **74**.9-11

casinos **129**.2

  new, UK **129**.15, 34

Volume numbers appear first (in bold) followed by page numbers; a change in volume number is preceded by a semi-colon.

Vol. **74** Money Matters

Vol. **76** The Water Crisis

Vol. **78** Threatened Species

Vol. **81** Alternative Therapies

Vol. **82** Protecting our Privacy

Vol. **85** The Housing Crisis

Vol. **88** Food and Nutrition

Vol. **89** Refugees

Vol. **96** Preventing Sexual Diseases

Vol. **97** Energy Matters

Vol. **99** Exploited Children

Vol. **100** Stress and Anxiety

Vol. **103** Animal Rights

Vol. **106** Trends in Marriage

Vol. **107** Work Issues

Vol. **115** Racial Discrimination

Vol. **116** Grief and Loss

Vol. **117** Self-Esteem and Body Image

Vol. **118** Focus on Sport

Vol. **119** Transport Trends

Vol. **120** The Human Rights Issue

Vol. **121** The Censorship Debate

Vol. **122** Bullying

Vol. **123** Young People and Health

Vol. **124** Parenting Issues

Vol. **125** Understanding Depression

Vol. **126** The Abortion Debate

Vol. **127** Eating Disorders

Vol. **128** The Cannabis Issue

Vol. **129** Gambling Trends

Vol. **130** Homelessness

Vol. **131** Citizenship and National Identity

Vol. **132** Child Abuse

Vol. **133** Teen Pregnancy and Lone Parents

Vol. **134** Customers and Consumerism

Vol. **135** Coping with Disability

Vol. **136** Self-Harm

Vol. **137** Crime and Anti-Social Behaviour

Vol. **138** A Genetically Modified Future?

Vol. **139** The Education Problem

Vol. **140** Vegetarian and Vegan Diets

Vol. **141** Mental Health

Vol. **142** Media Issues

Vol. **143** Problem Drinking

Vol. **144** The Cloning Debate

Vol. **145** Smoking Trends

Vol. **146** Sustainability and Environment

Vol. **147** The Terrorism Problem

Vol. **148** Religious Beliefs

Vol. **149** A Classless Society?

Vol. **150** Migration and Population

Vol. **151** Climate Change

Vol. **152** Euthanasia and the Right to Die

Vol. **153** Sexual Orientation and Society

Vol. **154** The Gender Gap

Vol. **155** Domestic Abuse

Vol. **156** Travel and Tourism

Vol. **157** The Problem of Globalisation

Vol. **158** The Internet Revolution

Vol. **159** An Ageing Population

Vol. **160** Poverty and Exclusion

Vol. **161** Waste Issues

Vol. **162** Staying Fit

Vol. **163** Drugs in the UK

supercasino **129.**14-16, 34
Catholic Church
    and abortion **126.**2, 36
    and euthanasia **152.**11, 29
    and contraception **126.**1-2
    and faith schools **148.**35
cattle
    cloning **144.**36-8
    and hybrid embryos **144.**11
CCTV (Closed Circuit Television) **82.**1, 6
    and crime prevention **82.**2, 3, 6
    and human rights **82.**24
    and RFID tags **82.**16
    statistics **82.**2
    and surveillance of public places **82.**3; **120.**33
    and workplace monitoring **82.**26, 27; **120.**32-3
cell ageing **159.**1
cell culture **103.**14, 18, 19
cell nuclear replacement **144.**15
censorship **121.**1-2
    films **121.**22, 23-5
    and the Internet **121.**18-21; **158.**37
    television **121.**36-7
census **150.**36
    ethnic group questions **115.**3
    religious affiliation results **148.**6-7
cereals **88.**5-6, 15
cerebral palsy and learning disabilities **135.**34
challenges as way of raising self-esteem **117.**33
challenging racism **115.**2
    at work **115.**12
charitable giving **130.**32, 33
charity foundation as remembrance **116.**17
chatrooms
    and bullying **122.**19-20, 21
    and sexual offences **158.**35
chavs
    children's perceptions of **149.**10-11
    prejudice against **149.**8
cheese and vegetarian diets **140.**6, 18, 22, 26
chemical/biological incidents, response to **147.**31
chemicals, disposal **161.**23
child abuse **120.**14-15; **132.**1-6
    abusers *see* child abusers
    care after abuse **132.**5
    definition **132.**1, 4
    and dependency **141.**10
    and dissociative disorders **141.**12-13
    effects of **132.**3, 4-5, 6, 22, 23
    emotional **132.**1, 5-6
        signs of **132.**4-5
    and false memory syndrome **132.**34-5
    and low self-esteem **117.**7-8
    and mental health problems **141.**10, 12-13
    neglect **132.**1-2
        signs of **132.**4-5
    online **132.**33
        images **132.**31-2
    physical **132.**1
        signs of **132.**4
    and the police **132.**3

signs of **132.**4-5
    telling someone about the abuse **132.**23-4, 28
child abusers **132.**2, 4, 22
    children as **132.**29, 30
    help for **132.**36-9
    misconceptions about **132.**25
child labour **99.**1-15; **120.**18-20
    and age of child **99.**2
    attitudes to **99.**1
    combating **99.**11-13
    defining **99.**2, 3
    demand for **99.**3
    domestic work **99.**1, 4, 7-10
    economic benefits of eliminating **99.**1, 6, 15
    economic truths of **99.**14-15
    and education **99.**3, 7, 10, 11-12, 15
    and human rights **99.**4, 6
    impact on a child **99.**2, 3
    legislation and laws
        enforcement of **99.**11
        improving **99.**11
    organisations to take action against **99.**4
    and poverty **99.**2, 3, 4, 11, 12, 14-15
    reasons for **99.**1, 2-3, 3-4
    statistics **99.**1, 2, 14
    suitability for certain types of work **99.**4
    types of **99.**1, 2, 3, 4
child mortality, Milliennium Goals **160.**31
child participation, and children's rights **120.**9-11
child pornography **99.**1, 16, 17, 20, 24, 25
    online **132.**31-2
    viewed by young people **132.**30
child poverty **106.**3; **160.**2, 3, 11, 19, 25, 29
    public attitudes to **160.**14
    and education **160.**16-22
    and family debt **160.**12
    and women's poverty **160.**15
child prostitution **99.**1, 16, 17, 25-6, 27-8
child protection **120.**14-15; **132.**3, 5
child psychiatrists **100.**2
child safety concerns of parents **124.**13-14
child sex tourism **156.**37-9
child soldiers **99.**1, 4, 29-39; **120.**20
    age of **99.**29-30
    benefits of ending child soldier use **99.**39
    defining **99.**29
    girls **99.**29, 31, 36
    harmful effects of being **99.**31, 36
    and human rights atrocities **99.**30
    and non-governmental armed groups **99.**30
    statistics **99.**29
Child Support Agency **133.**34, 37
    problems **124.**35; **133.**30
Child Tax Credit (CTC) **133.**33
childbirth
    deaths in **154.**12
    and exercise **162.**32
childcare
    advice **133.**37-8
    costs **124.**3
    emergency childcare **107.**22

experience for teenagers **133**.27
and fathers **124**.7-10, 11
and flexible working **107**.12, 16, 21, 23
and grandmothers **124**.37-8
prohibition of physical punishment **132**.15
statistics **154**.30
childhood obesity **88**.3, 11; **127**.33, 36-7; **162**.6, 13-14, 25-9
effects of exercise **162**.28, 29
measurement in schools **127**.36
as neglect **162**.27
childhood problems
and dependency **141**.9-10
and low self-esteem **117**.7-8, 31, 32-3
and post traumatic stress disorder **141**.3
childlessness for financial reasons **124**.18
ChildLine
and bullying **122**.1, 2, 10, 12
and child abuse **132**.2-3
and domestic violence **155**.25
and eating disorders **127**.20-21
and racism **115**.1
and self-harm **123**.36-7
and stepfamily worries **124**.23
and suicide **123**.35
childminders, prohibition of physical punishment **132**.15
children
abuse *see* child abuse
and advertising **134**.10, 12
age and children's rights **120**.5
alcohol consumption **143**.20
alcohol and mental health problems **125**.9
anti-extremism education **147**.34
attitudes to poverty **160**.4
and bereavement **116**.1, 9, 19-28
bereavement statistics **116**.20, 21
bereavement support **116**.15, 28
and body image **117**.14, 19, 22, 25
books showing gay couples **153**.19-20
in care, educational disadvantages **160**.22
as carers **135**.10-12
and censorship
films **121**.23-5

video games **121**.32-3
videos **121**.26
childhood leukaemia and medical research **103**.12
of cohabiting couples **106**.21-2; **124**.22
communication trends **158**.4
and consumerism **134**.11-12
costs of raising **124**.3; **134**.25
and criminal justice **137**.11-12
cycling **119**.28, 30
death
children's questions about **116**.26-7
children's understanding of **116**.22
and depression **123**.27-8; **125**.27-8
in developing countries
deaths and diseases from water-related illness **76**.2, 3, 5, 9, 13, 14
and global water supplies **76**.13-14
and hygiene education **76**.14
and sanitation provision **76**.13-14
and water collection **76**.13, 19-20
developing responsibility **124**.13-14
disabled *see* disabled children
discipline *see* discipline
and divorce **106**.27, 33-8; **124**.24, 29-30, 32-4
and domestic violence **155**.1, 4, 5, 19-25
drug awareness **163**.27
and eating disorders **127**.3, 20-21
ethnic minorities, and education **115**.18, 19-21
exercise, lack of **162**.13, 15, 25
falling out with parents **124**.18
and fathers **124**.7-11
and food advertising **88**.10, 11, 20, 35, 37
and food in school **123**.32
and funerals **116**.23, 26
and gambling
online gambling **129**.18
protection by Gambling Commission **129**.4
Scotland **129**.32-3
of gay couples **153**.20-22
gender development **154**.1
and grief **116**.19-28
health

Volume numbers appear first (in bold) followed by page numbers; a change in volume number is preceded by a semi-colon.

Vol. **74** Money Matters
Vol. **76** The Water Crisis
Vol. **78** Threatened Species
Vol. **81** Alternative Therapies
Vol. **82** Protecting our Privacy
Vol. **85** The Housing Crisis
Vol. **88** Food and Nutrition
Vol. **89** Refugees
Vol. **96** Preventing Sexual Diseases
Vol. **97** Energy Matters
Vol. **99** Exploited Children
Vol. **100** Stress and Anxiety
Vol. **103** Animal Rights
Vol. **106** Trends in Marriage
Vol. **107** Work Issues
Vol. **115** Racial Discrimination
Vol. **116** Grief and Loss
Vol. **117** Self-Esteem and Body Image
Vol. **118** Focus on Sport
Vol. **119** Transport Trends
Vol. **120** The Human Rights Issue
Vol. **121** The Censorship Debate

Vol. **122** Bullying
Vol. **123** Young People and Health
Vol. **124** Parenting Issues
Vol. **125** Understanding Depression
Vol. **126** The Abortion Debate
Vol. **127** Eating Disorders
Vol. **128** The Cannabis Issue
Vol. **129** Gambling Trends
Vol. **130** Homelessness
Vol. **131** Citizenship and National Identity
Vol. **132** Child Abuse
Vol. **133** Teen Pregnancy and Lone Parents
Vol. **134** Customers and Consumerism
Vol. **135** Coping with Disability
Vol. **136** Self-Harm
Vol. **137** Crime and Anti-Social Behaviour
Vol. **138** A Genetically Modified Future?
Vol. **139** The Education Problem
Vol. **140** Vegetarian and Vegan Diets
Vol. **141** Mental Health
Vol. **142** Media Issues
Vol. **143** Problem Drinking

Vol. **144** The Cloning Debate
Vol. **145** Smoking Trends
Vol. **146** Sustainability and Environment
Vol. **147** The Terrorism Problem
Vol. **148** Religious Beliefs
Vol. **149** A Classless Society?
Vol. **150** Migration and Population
Vol. **151** Climate Change
Vol. **152** Euthanasia and the Right to Die
Vol. **153** Sexual Orientation and Society
Vol. **154** The Gender Gap
Vol. **155** Domestic Abuse
Vol. **156** Travel and Tourism
Vol. **157** The Problem of Globalisation
Vol. **158** The Internet Revolution
Vol. **159** An Ageing Population
Vol. **160** Poverty and Exclusion
Vol. **161** Waste Issues
Vol. **162** Staying Fit
Vol. **163** Drugs in the UK

government strategy **162**.17
   and transport **119**.13-14, 31
healthy weight **162**.25
and HIV/AIDS **96**.20, 39
and homelessness **130**.23
and the Internet **158**.20-21, 27-30
of lone parents **124**.33-4; **133**.28, 31
and media violence **121**.33, 34, 35
and mental health
   mental health problems **125**.16; **141**.1, 20-21
   mental health programmes **141**.37
   effect of parents' mental health problems **141**.24-5
and mobile phone tracking **82**.19, 20
and money matters **74**.6-7, 12-13
needs **120**.2
naming after brands **134**.12
obesity *see* childhood obesity
online gaming addiction **158**.39
and passive smoking **145**.2, 28-9
and poverty *see* child poverty
and prison *see* youth custody
and racism **115**.1-2, 9
refugees **89**.39; **120**.21-2
and road accidents **119**.5, 28, 30-31
and road safety **119**.5-6
safety concerns of parents **124**.13-14; **137**.20
sex education **133**.15, 17
sexual abuse *see* sexual abuse
smacking *see* smacking
and smoking **123**.11-13; **145**.2-3
   attitudes to smoking **145**.20
   health effects **145**.2
   and the law **145**.3
   mother smoking in pregnancy **145**.32-3
   effects of nicotine **145**.27
   passive smoking **145**.2, 28-9
social differences, perceptions of **149**.9-12
and stepfamilies **124**.23-8
and suicide **123**.35
of teenage mothers **133**.10
and television
   parental control of viewing **121**.26, 27, 34
and terrorism **147**.32
time spent with parents **106**.2
   fathers **124**.7-8, 9, 11
travel to school **119**.26, 29-30
and video classification **121**.32-3
and video games **121**.32-3
and women's earnings **154**.35-6
children's rights **120**.1-22
and age of children **120**.1, 2
and child abuse **120**.14-15
and children's needs **120**.2
and justice system **120**.1-2, 12-13
and participation in decision-making **120**.9-11
refugees **120**.21-2
and responsibilities **120**.1
timeline **120**.3
to vote **120**.7-8
in the UK **120**.2
UN Convention on the Rights of the Child **120**.4-6

chimeras **144**.10-12
Chinese medicine **81**.2, 3
   and cancer **81**.33
   and endangered species **81**.15
   herbal medicine **81**.14-15, 39
chiropractic **81**.8-9, 23, 36
   effectiveness of **81**.24
   misdiagnosis and dangers of **81**.23, 24
   regulation of **81**.23
   and scientists **81**.28, 29
chlamydia **96**.2-3, 4, 9; **123**.26
   and HIV **96**.12
   increase in cases of **96**.8, 10
   signs and symptoms **96**.5
   testing for **96**.2, 3, 5
   treatment **96**.5
chocolate **88**.18-19, 31
   vegan **140**.22, 26
choice as consumer right **134**.1
cholera **76**.2, 12, 13, 32
Christianity **148**.2
   and abortion and contraception **126**.1-2
   and the Census (2001) **148**.6, 7
   and church attendance **148**.7, 18-19, 20-21, 23, 27
   degree of commitment **148**.7
   denominations **148**.6
   discrimination against **148**.28
   festivals **148**.2
   and food culture **148**.10
   funerals **116**.33
church attendance **148**.7, 18-19, 20-21, 23, 27
   effect on young people **137**.26
Church of England
   and abortion and contraception **126**.1
   baptisms **148**.22
   and euthanasia **152**.34
   and faith schools **148**.35
   and marriage **106**.9-10
   as state religion (established church) **148**.21-2
Church of Scotland and ethics of human cloning **144**.5-6
cider, strength of **143**.1
cigarettes
   chemicals in **145**.1
   cost **145**.3, 17
   pack size **145**.19
   sales, effect of smoking ban **145**.16-17
cities *see* cars, congestion; urban areas; urban growth
citizen photojournalism **142**.23
Citizens Advice Bureaux, debt advice **134**.23
citizenship **89**.37
   British identity **131**.1-14
   European Union **131**.38
   global **131**.37
   government **131**.15-25
   survey **131**.2-3
   test **131**.12
   young people **131**.26-39
Citizenship Education in schools **131**.36
city colleges and special educational needs **135**.36
civic involvement, young people **131**.31-2
civil law **137**.1

civil liberties

and media regulation **142**.1-2

civil partnerships **153**.26-30

numbers **153**.29-30

and parental responsibility **153**.33

Civil Partnerships Act **153**.26-8

civil protest **121**.14

civil wars **89**.7-8

CJD (Creutzfeld Jacob disease) **141**.7

class *see* social class

class A drugs

young people's use **163**.26-7

class sizes (schools) **139**.1, 12

classification

of drugs **128**.26; **163**.2, 31, 33-4, 37

of films **121**.22, 23-5, 29-30

of video games **121**.32-3

cleaner fuels **119**.20-23

clearing (university entrance) **139**.30

clenbuterol hydrochloride **118**.35

climate change

benefits **151**.6

and biodiversity **146**.19, 21

and British tourism **156**.28

and consumerism **134**.31

controversies **151**.3-6

denial of **151**.12-13, 14-15

effects of **151**.1, 6, 8, 9, 10

and food production **140**.17, 37

and forests **146**.30

and global water supplies **76**.1, 3, 5, 8

and globalisation **157**.10

hypocrisy about **151**.12-13

and inequality **151**.11, 19

and meat production **140**.17

natural **151**.3

and nuclear power **97**.19-20, 21, 22

political action **151**.16-17, 27

and population control **151**.31-2

public action **151**. 38-9

public awareness of factors contributing to **97**.34

and renewable energy sources

bioenergy **97**.18

case for **97**.1-2

and wind energy **97**.15

and species extinction **78**.10, 11

and tourism **156**.1, 25

tourist attitudes to **156**.28-30

and transport emissions **119**.14, 30

and water management **76**.34

climate models **151**.5

cloning

animals **144**.30-39

definition **144**.1, 4, 5, 18

ethical issues **144**.2-3, 5-6, 7-8

and factory farming **144**.35

and food production **144**.36-9

how it works **144**.1, 4, 14

human **144**.1-14

natural **144**.1

regulations **144**.3

risks **144**.2, 3, 6, 8

clothes, recycling **161**.28

CO_2 *see* carbon dioxide

co-parenting after divorce **124**.32

coaches, sports

female **118**.20

and pressure to use drugs **118**.29

coal

and carbon allowances **151**.37

as an energy source **97**.4

coastal areas, effect of climate change **151**.10

cocaine **163**.4

street sales **163**.12

use prevalence **163**.7, 25

worldwide production **163**.25

cocoa industry and child labour **120**.19

coffee growers and fairtrade **157**.32, 33

cognitive ability and gender **154**.24

Cognitive Behavioural Therapy (CBT) **141**.35

and bipolar disorder **141**.14-15

for bulimia nervosa (CBT-BN) **127**.14

and giving up cannabis use **128**.10

and self-harm **136**.11

Volume numbers appear first (in bold) followed by page numbers; a change in volume number is preceded by a semi-colon.

Vol. **74** Money Matters
Vol. **76** The Water Crisis
Vol. **78** Threatened Species
Vol. **81** Alternative Therapies
Vol. **82** Protecting our Privacy
Vol. **85** The Housing Crisis
Vol. **88** Food and Nutrition
Vol. **89** Refugees
Vol. **96** Preventing Sexual Diseases
Vol. **97** Energy Matters
Vol. **99** Exploited Children
Vol. **100** Stress and Anxiety
Vol. **103** Animal Rights
Vol. **106** Trends in Marriage
Vol. **107** Work Issues
Vol. **115** Racial Discrimination
Vol. **116** Grief and Loss
Vol. **117** Self-Esteem and Body Image
Vol. **118** Focus on Sport
Vol. **119** Transport Trends
Vol. **120** The Human Rights Issue
Vol. **121** The Censorship Debate

Vol. **122** Bullying
Vol. **123** Young People and Health
Vol. **124** Parenting Issues
Vol. **125** Understanding Depression
Vol. **126** The Abortion Debate
Vol. **127** Eating Disorders
Vol. **128** The Cannabis Issue
Vol. **129** Gambling Trends
Vol. **130** Homelessness
Vol. **131** Citizenship and National Identity
Vol. **132** Child Abuse
Vol. **133** Teen Pregnancy and Lone Parents
Vol. **134** Customers and Consumerism
Vol. **135** Coping with Disability
Vol. **136** Self-Harm
Vol. **137** Crime and Anti-Social Behaviour
Vol. **138** A Genetically Modified Future?
Vol. **139** The Education Problem
Vol. **140** Vegetarian and Vegan Diets
Vol. **141** Mental Health
Vol. **142** Media Issues
Vol. **143** Problem Drinking

Vol. **144** The Cloning Debate
Vol. **145** Smoking Trends
Vol. **146** Sustainability and Environment
Vol. **147** The Terrorism Problem
Vol. **148** Religious Beliefs
Vol. **149** A Classless Society?
Vol. **150** Migration and Population
Vol. **151** Climate Change
Vol. **152** Euthanasia and the Right to Die
Vol. **153** Sexual Orientation and Society
Vol. **154** The Gender Gap
Vol. **155** Domestic Abuse
Vol. **156** Travel and Tourism
Vol. **157** The Problem of Globalisation
Vol. **158** The Internet Revolution
Vol. **159** An Ageing Population
Vol. **160** Poverty and Exclusion
Vol. **161** Waste Issues
Vol. **162** Staying Fit
Vol. **163** Drugs in the UK

and Seasonal Affective Disorder 125.38
cohabitation
    age at first 106.10
    changing views on 106.4
    and stability for children 124.22
    and 'common law' marriages 106.8
    legal protection for cohabitees 106.7-8, 10
    and likelihood of marriage 106.5
    reasons for 106.11
    and splitting up 106.21
collagen, stem cell therapy 144.21-2
colour as grounds for discrimination 115.7
coming out 153.3, 8
commercial sexual exploitation of children 156.38-9
commercialization
    effect on children 134.11-12
    in sport 118.9
'common law' marriages 106.8, 9-10
communication
    and abortion 126.11
    importance in bereavement 116.24-5
    importance in depression 125.3, 39
      young people 125.8
    and eating disorders 127.30
    and self-esteem 117.4
    trends 158.4-6
Communications Act and media mergers 142.4
communications data 82.5, 33-4
    government monitoring of 82.1-2
    and the law 82.33-4
communities
    and identity cards 82.11
    sustainable 85.32, 38, 39
community arts 141.38
community cohesion 131.2
community involvement, young people 131.32
community sentences 137.12
compensation for faulty goods 134.2, 17
competition
    and consumer choice 134.1
    telecommunications industry 158.6
competition scams 134.26
competitive sport in schools 118.4
complaints
    about goods 134.2, 17
complementary medicine (CM)
    and consumer choice 81.37
    and consumer ignorance 81.35
    defining 81.1, 4
    and depression 125.39
      manic depression 125.20
    and diagnosis 81.34
    disciplines within 81.1-3
    effectiveness of 81.22-4, 26, 27, 31
    expenditure on 81.23, 37, 39
    and GPs 81.21
    impact on wildlife 78.23
    and misdiagnosis 81.23
    and multiple sclerosis 81.30-1
    and the placebo effect 81.26, 28, 34
    regulation of 81.23

    safety of 81.27, 31
    and scientists 81.28-9
    and self-care 81.36-7
    why bogus therapies seem to work 81.34
complex carbohydrates 88.2
composting waste 161.19, 28-9, 30
compulsions (obsessional rituals) 141.17
compulsive eating 127.20-21
compulsive exercise 162.39
compulsive gambling 129.2, 27-39
    causes 129.29
    definition 129.11
    drug treatment 129.39
    and Gambling Commission 129.5
    help for 129.5, 29, 36, 37, 39
    online gambling 129.21-2
    signs 129.28, 29, 35-6, 38
    support groups 129.37
    under 16s 129.13, 25, 32-3
    women 129.34
compulsive shopping 134.13, 14
compulsory admission for eating disorders 127.29
compulsory turnout to vote 131.20-21
computer games
    violence, influence on children 121.32-3, 35
computer research, in medicine 103.13-14, 17, 19, 22
computers
    and euthanasia decision-making 152.38-9
    home computer ownership 134.5
    recycling 161.29
    spyware as tool of domestic abuse 155.15-16
conception 123.22; 133.8
    rate, young people 126.30-31; 133.2
condoms 123.23
    availability of 96.2
    and HIV 96.12, 14, 16, 24, 25, 29, 30, 32, 33, 34
    and the prevention of STIs 96.1-2, 9; 123.24, 25
confidence
    self-confidence see self-esteem
confidentiality
    and abortion 126.13, 28, 29
      effect on teenage conception rate 126.30
    and eating disorders 127.28
congenital adrenal hyperplasia 154.1
congestion, traffic 119.11
    congestion charging 119.12, 34-5, 38
    rail 119.35
    and road building 119.12
conservation
    animal species 78.11
    English environment 146.32-3
    and the exotic pet trade 78.21-2
    plant species 78.17
    tree species 78.12
    zoo conservation 78.24-5
Conservative party
    and GM crops 138.39
    policies on crime 137.2
construction industry
    and energy efficiency 97.36
    sustainability 146.11

waste recycling **161**.23
consultancies, tourism **156**.9
consumer adultery **161**.8-9
consumer assurance **134**.33-4
consumer choice **134**.1
consumer credit debt **134**.4, 23
consumer durables **134**.3-4, 5
consumer organisations **134**.21
consumer rights **134**.1-2, 17-21
    faulty goods **134**.2, 17
    and guarantees **134**.18-19
    private sales and auctions **134**.20
    and safety **134**.2
    secondhand goods **134**.20
consumer spending **134**.3-4
consumerism
    green consumerism **146**.38-9
    and mental health problems **134**.5
consumers **134**.1
    and animal welfare **140**.31, 33
    and child labour **99**.12
    ethical behaviour **134**.33-5
    and genetic modification **138**.9
    older people **159**.19
    and RFID tags **82**.16-17, 35
    rights *see* consumer rights
    satisfaction **134**.6
    spending *see* consumer spending
consumption
    sustainable **146**.7
    UK **150**.32
contained (indoor) GMOs **138**.12
contamination
    groundwater **146**.36
    land **146**.22
content sharing sites **142**.35
contraception **123**.22-3
    advice **126**.23-4
    'double dutch' method of **96**.2
    emergency contraception (EC) **126**.24
    and men **96**.13
    and microbicides **96**.34

    religious views **126**.1-3
    and young people **123**.22-3; **133**.1, 2, 17
contract sales **107**.22
control orders **147**.3
copycat behaviour, self-harm **136**.10
copyright
    and downloading **158**.35, 36
    and Freedom of Information Act **142**.19
coral trade **78**.21
coronary heart disease (CHD) *see* heart disease
coroner **116**.32
corporal punishment **132**.7-21
    abolishing **132**.13
    and children's rights **120**.15
    effects of **132**.9-10, 13
    and human rights **132**.9, 12-13, 16-17
    ineffectiveness **132**.9
    legal position **132**.15
    prevalence of **132**.15-16
    in schools, globally **132**.7
    as stress relief for adults **132**.10
cosmetic testing on animals **103**.23
cosmetic surgery **117**.21, 24-5
    and ethnicity **117**.29-30
    and stem cell therapy **144**.24-5
costs
    of abortion **126**.12
    academies **139**.15
    of ageing **159**.19-30
    of alcohol, effect on consumption **143**.17, 31
    of alcohol misuse **143**.36
    of the asylum system **89**.11, 30
    of cannabis **128**.2, 6
    of child poverty **160**.11
    of civil partnerships **153**.28
    of cleaner vehicles **119**.20-24
    of crime **137**.2
    of dementia **159**.35
    of disability **135**.5, 17, 18
    of domestic violence **155**.25
    of education **139**.1, 35; **160**.16-17, 19
    of fly-tipping **161**.16

Volume numbers appear first (in bold) followed by page numbers; a change in volume number is preceded by a semi-colon.

Vol. **74** Money Matters
Vol. **76** The Water Crisis
Vol. **78** Threatened Species
Vol. **81** Alternative Therapies
Vol. **82** Protecting our Privacy
Vol. **85** The Housing Crisis
Vol. **88** Food and Nutrition
Vol. **89** Refugees
Vol. **96** Preventing Sexual Diseases
Vol. **97** Energy Matters
Vol. **99** Exploited Children
Vol. **100** Stress and Anxiety
Vol. **103** Animal Rights
Vol. **106** Trends in Marriage
Vol. **107** Work Issues
Vol. **115** Racial Discrimination
Vol. **116** Grief and Loss
Vol. **117** Self-Esteem and Body Image
Vol. **118** Focus on Sport
Vol. **119** Transport Trends
Vol. **120** The Human Rights Issue
Vol. **121** The Censorship Debate

Vol. **122** Bullying
Vol. **123** Young People and Health
Vol. **124** Parenting Issues
Vol. **125** Understanding Depression
Vol. **126** The Abortion Debate
Vol. **127** Eating Disorders
Vol. **128** The Cannabis Issue
Vol. **129** Gambling Trends
Vol. **130** Homelessness
Vol. **131** Citizenship and National Identity
Vol. **132** Child Abuse
Vol. **133** Teen Pregnancy and Lone Parents
Vol. **134** Customers and Consumerism
Vol. **135** Coping with Disability
Vol. **136** Self-Harm
Vol. **137** Crime and Anti-Social Behaviour
Vol. **138** A Genetically Modified Future?
Vol. **139** The Education Problem
Vol. **140** Vegetarian and Vegan Diets
Vol. **141** Mental Health
Vol. **142** Media Issues
Vol. **143** Problem Drinking

Vol. **144** The Cloning Debate
Vol. **145** Smoking Trends
Vol. **146** Sustainability and Environment
Vol. **147** The Terrorism Problem
Vol. **148** Religious Beliefs
Vol. **149** A Classless Society?
Vol. **150** Migration and Population
Vol. **151** Climate Change
Vol. **152** Euthanasia and the Right to Die
Vol. **153** Sexual Orientation and Society
Vol. **154** The Gender Gap
Vol. **155** Domestic Abuse
Vol. **156** Travel and Tourism
Vol. **157** The Problem of Globalisation
Vol. **158** The Internet Revolution
Vol. **159** An Ageing Population
Vol. **160** Poverty and Exclusion
Vol. **161** Waste Issues
Vol. **162** Staying Fit
Vol. **163** Drugs in the UK

of fuel **160**.22-3
of global warming **151**.8
of home care for the elderly **159**.26
of identity cards **120**.35-6; **131**.13
of imprisonment **137**.37
of mental health problems **125**.16
of motoring **119**.14
of obesity **127**.33-4, 37
of psychological therapy **125**.7
of raising a child **124**.3
    as reason for smaller families **124**.18
of smoking **145**.3, 17, 38
of social exclusion **149**.39
of solicitors **137**.36
university degrees **139**.35
of vegan diet **140**.25
of wasted food **161**.10-11
of zero emission fuels **151**.28-9
cotinine **145**.26
cotton
    fairtrade **157**.28, 34
    genetically modified **138**.35
council tax
    benefit **135**.5
    and civil partnerships **153**.28
    lone parents **133**.35, 38
counselling **141**.35
    for alcohol abuse **143**.25, 38
    for childhood bullying **122**.6
    for depression **125**.30-31
    eating disorders **127**.21, 29
    and help with stress **100**.32, 34
    for post-natal depression **125**.18
    for sexual abuse **132**.24
    and testing for HIV **96**.1
counter-terrorism **147**.2, 26-39
    and online activities **147**.9
    targeting terrorist funds **147**.3, 28-9
    UK strategy **147**.28-9
country of birth *see* birth country
countryside, and the production and use of energy **97**.24-5
county courts **137**.36
coursework and Internet plagiarism **158**.19-20
courts of law
    children's access to **120**.1-2
    court hearings **137**.36
    and debts **74**.35
    and torture evidence **120**.39
cows *see* cattle
crack cocaine **163**.4
cranial osteopathy **81**.2
creationism **148**.37
    teaching 36
creativity
    and help for self-harm **136**.3
    and mental health **141**.38
credit
    advantages and disadvantages of **74**.23
    bank overdrafts **74**.1, 18, 19, 21-2
    consumer credit levels **134**.4, 23, 24
    credit ratings **74**.25, 27

and homeless young people **130**.25-6
    interest rates **74**.23
    obtaining **74**.23
    and students **74**.30
    types of **134**.22
    using wisely **134**.22
credit cards **74**.26-7; **134**.22, 24
    and the cashless society **74**.9-11
    and consumer rights **134**.18
    credit reference agencies **74**.25, 27
    interest rates **74**.26, 27
    limits **74**.26
    minimum repayments **74**.26
    'payment holidays' **74**.26
    shopping around for **74**.25-6
    store cards **74**.27
    and students **74**.3, 30, 32, 36, 37
    theft, and RFID tags **82**.16
    and young people **74**.15, 16, 23
cremation **116**.37-8
crime
    controlling movement of criminals in EU **150**.7
    costs of **137**.2; **149**.39
    cybercrime **158**.35
    definition **137**.1, 3
    detection rates **137**.3-4
    and divorce **106**.31
    and domestic violence **155**.2
    and drugs **163**.2-3, 23
    and educational underachievement **149**.39
    Europe **137**.6
    fear of **137**.5, 7; **159**.3
    filesharing **158**.36
    and forced marriages **155**.17
    and identity cards
        forging **82**.7, 8
        as a means of combating crime **82**.7, 8, 10, 11
    identity theft **158**.3
    and licensing hours change **143**.23
    and the media **137**.2
    and migrants **150**.12, 13, 14
    and mobile phones **158**.12-13
    non-reporting, reasons for **137**.31
    phishing **158**.36
    public worry about **137**.5, 7
    racially motivated **115**.9-10
    religiously motivated **115**.27; **148**.29
    reporting **137**.28, 30-31
    and RFID cards **82**.17
    statistics **137**.3-4
    and surveillance **82**.17-18
    trends **137**.1, 4
    victims of *see* victims of crime
    victim personal statement **137**.31
    Wi-Fi hijacking **158**.37
    wildlife **78**.19, 38-9
    youth crime, costs of **149**.39
crime prevention and CCTV **82**.2, 3, 6
criminal injuries compensation **137**.28
criminal justice bill **137**.29-30
criminal justice system

and children's rights **120**.12
and domestic violence **155**.35-8
and gender equality **154**.4
and young offenders **137**.12, 17
criminal offences **137**.1
criminal responsibility, age of **137**.11, 13
criminality
and high self-esteem **117**.7
and mental health problems **125**.16
crisis services, manic depression **125**.20
criticism **117**.2-3
crocodile farming **140**.30
crop biotechnology *see* genetically modified (GM) crops
crop rotation **88**.14
cross-contamination, genetic **138**.4
cross-cultural communication **142**.34
cross-dressing **153**.13
cross-pollination, GM and non-GM crops **138**.6-7, 12-13
Crown Court **137**.36
cruises **156**.1-2
crystal meth (methamphetamine) **163**.16-17, 32
crystal healing **81**.2
CSA problems, single parent families **124**.35
cultural capital **149**.2
cultural Christianity **148**.23-5
cultural differences and mixed-faith relationships **115**.39
cultural traditions
British **131**.1
and children's rights **120**.2
culture
and biological environment **146**.19
and corporal punishment **132**.10
and domestic violence **155**.4
and gender discrimination **154**.13-14
and health inequalities **149**.14
and the media **142**.34
and religion **126**.1; **148**.23-5
effect of tourism **156**.22
curfew orders **137**.12
custody *see* prison; youth custody
customer service satisfaction **134**.6
customs, drugs seizures **163**.37

cuts, first aid **136**.22-3
cutting (self-harm), safety measures **136**.22
cyanovirin-N **138**.22
cyber-bullying **122**.19-26
cybercrime **158**.35
cyberterrorism **147**.8-9
cybrids (animal-human hybrids) **144**.9, 10-12
cycle of abuse **132**.25
cycling **119**.25, 29
children **119**.28; **124**.14
health benefits **119**.39
helmets **119**.28
to school **119**.30
cystic fibrosis research, animal experimentation **144**.34

D

D&E (surgical dilation and evacuation) **126**.10, 14
DAB digital radio **158**.5
daily benchmarks for alcohol consumption **143**.8, 25, 26-7, 34
awareness of **143**.11, 34
dairy foods **88**.6, 15
dairy-free diet **140**.22-3, 26
dark tourism **156**.35-6
data protection
communications data **82**.33-4
and RFID tags **82**.16
and self-regulation **82**.5
Data Protection Acts **82**.21-2, 37-8, 39
day centres for homeless people **130**.31
daylight, effect on mental health **141**.35
death sites as tourist venues **156**.35-6
death tourism **152**.16
deaths
alcohol-related **143**.3, 6, 37
cancer **81**.23, 32
of children
cyclists **119**.28
pedestrians **119**.5, 30
children's questions about death **116**.26-7
children's understanding of death **116**.22

Volume numbers appear first (in bold) followed by page numbers; a change in volume number is preceded by a semi-colon.

Vol. **74** Money Matters
Vol. **76** The Water Crisis
Vol. **78** Threatened Species
Vol. **81** Alternative Therapies
Vol. **82** Protecting our Privacy
Vol. **85** The Housing Crisis
Vol. **88** Food and Nutrition
Vol. **89** Refugees
Vol. **96** Preventing Sexual Diseases
Vol. **97** Energy Matters
Vol. **99** Exploited Children
Vol. **100** Stress and Anxiety
Vol. **103** Animal Rights
Vol. **106** Trends in Marriage
Vol. **107** Work Issues
Vol. **115** Racial Discrimination
Vol. **116** Grief and Loss
Vol. **117** Self-Esteem and Body Image
Vol. **118** Focus on Sport
Vol. **119** Transport Trends
Vol. **120** The Human Rights Issue
Vol. **121** The Censorship Debate

Vol. **122** Bullying
Vol. **123** Young People and Health
Vol. **124** Parenting Issues
Vol. **125** Understanding Depression
Vol. **126** The Abortion Debate
Vol. **127** Eating Disorders
Vol. **128** The Cannabis Issue
Vol. **129** Gambling Trends
Vol. **130** Homelessness
Vol. **131** Citizenship and National Identity
Vol. **132** Child Abuse
Vol. **133** Teen Pregnancy and Lone Parents
Vol. **134** Customers and Consumerism
Vol. **135** Coping with Disability
Vol. **136** Self-Harm
Vol. **137** Crime and Anti-Social Behaviour
Vol. **138** A Genetically Modified Future?
Vol. **139** The Education Problem
Vol. **140** Vegetarian and Vegan Diets
Vol. **141** Mental Health
Vol. **142** Media Issues
Vol. **143** Problem Drinking

Vol. **144** The Cloning Debate
Vol. **145** Smoking Trends
Vol. **146** Sustainability and Environment
Vol. **147** The Terrorism Problem
Vol. **148** Religious Beliefs
Vol. **149** A Classless Society?
Vol. **150** Migration and Population
Vol. **151** Climate Change
Vol. **152** Euthanasia and the Right to Die
Vol. **153** Sexual Orientation and Society
Vol. **154** The Gender Gap
Vol. **155** Domestic Abuse
Vol. **156** Travel and Tourism
Vol. **157** The Problem of Globalisation
Vol. **158** The Internet Revolution
Vol. **159** An Ageing Population
Vol. **160** Poverty and Exclusion
Vol. **161** Waste Issues
Vol. **162** Staying Fit
Vol. **163** Drugs in the UK

and cohabitation **106**.8
and drug misuse **163**.11-12
formal procedures **116**.29-32
in hospital **116**.31
older people, winter **159**.4
registering **116**.31
in road accidents **119**.4, 5, 30
from smoking **145**.1, 4, 12, 22, 24
unexpected **116**.31
from water-related diseases **76**.2, 9, 13, 14, 20, 35
debit cards **134**.24
and the cashless society **74**.9-11
and young people **74**.23-4
debt **134**.23-5; **160**.32-3
advice **134**.23, 25
attitudes to **74**.5
buying on credit **134**.22
calculating total repayments **74**.26
communication with creditors **74**.25
developing world **157**.5, 9-10; **160**.33
and families **74**.3, 5-6
getting out of **74**.16
and homeless young people **130**.24-6
managing **74**.34-5
and poverty **160**.12
and social class **149**.20
statistics **134**.4, 23, 24
students **74**.3, 5, 19-20, 31-2, 34-9; **134**.24
amounts of debt **74**.36
calculating essential expenditure **74**.34
coping with **74**.28-9, 34-5
court and summonses **74**.35
and credit cards **74**.3, 30, 32, 36, 37
maximising your income **74**.34
overdrafts **74**.1, 21-2
priority debts **74**.34-5
tips for cutting **74**.25-6
and unauthorised money lenders **74**.24
and young people **74**.1, 2, 15, 16, 23; **134**.24
debt crisis **157**.5
decision-making
children's participation in **120**.9-11
in euthanasia cases **152**.38-9
and self-esteem **117**.37
young people **131**.28
feelings of exclusion **131**.26
decontamination of land, by plants **138**.14
decriminalisation of cannabis **128**.7, 12
deer
as food **140**.15, 17
hunting **103**.24, 28, 29
deforestation **78**.11, 18; **146**.30-31
and water shortages **76**.21, 36
degrees, university
costs **139**.34, 35
courses **139**.2, 29, 30, 38-9
and earnings **139**.35, 36, 37
and ethnicity **139**.8
and gender **139**.10
results rising **139**.33
delinquency, effect of divorce **124**.34

dementia **141**.6-8; **159**.4, 35-9
and depression **125**.5
fear of **159**.39
statistics **125**.16
democracy
and extremism **131**.23-4
proposal for reform **131**.25
dental dams **96**.2
dependency **141**.9-10
depersonalisation **141**.11
deportation as anti-terrorism measure **120**.38-9
depressant drugs (downers) **163**.2, 5-6
alcohol **143**.4
depression **125**.1-23
and abortion **126**.11
and alcohol **125**.2, 3, 36-7; **143**.4
anti-depressant drugs *see* anti-depressant drugs
and cannabis use **128**.14
causes of **125**.2, 6, 19, 23
in children and young people **123**.27-8; **125**.8, 9, 27-8
and complementary therapies **81**.30, 31; **125**.20, 39
endogenous **125**.4
and exam stress **100**.7
and exercise **125**.3, 20, 39; **141**.39; **162**.37, 38
genetic factors in **125**.2
and grief **116**.5, 19
and incapacity benefit **100**.23
manic depression *see* bipolar affective disorder
and men **125**.13-15
in older people **125**.22-3
and personality **125**.2
and physical illness **125**.2, 5-6
post-natal **125**.4, 17-18
prevalence of **141**.1, 2
reactive **125**.4
seeking help **125**.2-3
and sexual abuse **132**.28
statistics on **136**.33
and stress **100**.1, 24
and suicide **125**.10
symptoms of **125**.1, 13
in the elderly **125**.22-3
manic depression **125**.19
post-natal depression **125**.17
seasonal affective disorder **125**.18
teenagers **125**.8
treatment of **125**.24-39
children and young people **125**.8, 27-8
diet **125**.3, 39
drugs **125**.7, 19, 22, 24-5, 32, 35
ECT (electroconvulsive therapy) **125**.25-6, 34, 35
elderly people **125**.23
manic depression **125**.19-20
post-natal depression **125**.17-18
psychotherapies **125**.29-31
Seasonal Affective Disorder **125**.18
self-help **125**.3, 39
talking therapies **125**.29-31
types of **125**.4
and underage drinking **125**.9
unipolar (endogenous) **125**.4, 10

deprived areas as tourist sights **156**.33-5
derealisation **141**.11
desertification
    causing migration **146**.16
    and water shortages **76**.21, 36
detention
    of children **120**.12; 17
    of refugee children **120**.21
designer holidays **156**.2
detention centres **89**.12, 13
    restraint techniques **120**.17
detoxification **143**.38
developing countries
    ageing populations **159**.5
    aid to *see* aid
    AIDS/HIV in **96**.17-18, 36-7
    alcohol consumption **143**.6
    child labour in **99**.1, 2
    and climate change action **151**.19
    damaging effects of recycling **161**.35
    debt and poverty **157**.9-10
    and disability **135**.25, 26-7
    effect of EU GM controls **138**.29-30
    and free trade **157**.20, 25, 26-7
    and gap years **156**.15-19
    and globalisation **157**.25
    and GM crops **138**.9, 10, 23, 34-5
    money deposits in UK **146**.6
    pensions **159**.24
    receiving unwanted waste **161**.37
    and the right to water **76**.24-5, 32
    and smoking **145**.22-4
    and tourism
        problems **156**.22
        slum tours **156**.33-5
        sustainable tourism **156**.22-3
        tourism dependency **156**.21
    water collection **76**.13, 19-20
    water pollution **76**.4, 10
    water and sanitation services **76**.7, 8, 12, 17, 21
    water shortages **76**.16, 19, 21
        and agriculture **76**.3, 4

    and aid programmes **76**.5
    statistics **76**.2, 6, 7
    and World Trade Organization **157**.22, 24
development
    effect on environment **146**.24
    and migration **150**.2
development aid, contributing to climate change **151**.27
devolution, effect on national identity **131**.5, 6
diabetes
    and complementary therapies **81**.21
    and obesity **127**.34
diarrhoea
    and access to safe water and sanitation **76**.17
    deaths from **76**.14, 30
    and hygiene promotion **76**.6, 12
    links to contaminated water **76**.5, 12
diet
    and Buddhism **148**. 11
    and cancer treatments **81**.32-3
    and child behaviour **120**.16
    and Christianity **148**.2, 10
    and depression **125**.3, 39
    dietary trends **125**.11-12
    healthy *see* healthy eating
    and Hinduism **148**.3, 11
    and Islam **148**.3-4, 11
    and Judaism **148**.4, 10-11
    and mental health **125**.11-12; **141**.30-31, 34
    and religion **148**.10-11
    and Seasonal Affective Disorder **125**.38
    and Sikhism **148**.5
    and stress **100**.19, 30, 31, 35
    teenage girls **117**.20, 21
    and weight loss **162**.2
    worldwide changes **162**.6
    young people **123**.1, 6-7; 31
dietary obsession (orthorexia nervosa) **127**.19
dieting
    girls and young women **117**.20-21
digital entertainment **158**.3, 5, 7, 21-2
digital radio **158**.5
digital television **158**.5

Volume numbers appear first (in bold) followed by page numbers; a change in volume number is preceded by a semi-colon.

Vol. **74** Money Matters
Vol. **76** The Water Crisis
Vol. **78** Threatened Species
Vol. **81** Alternative Therapies
Vol. **82** Protecting our Privacy
Vol. **85** The Housing Crisis
Vol. **88** Food and Nutrition
Vol. **89** Refugees
Vol. **96** Preventing Sexual Diseases
Vol. **97** Energy Matters
Vol. **99** Exploited Children
Vol. **100** Stress and Anxiety
Vol. **103** Animal Rights
Vol. **106** Trends in Marriage
Vol. **107** Work Issues
Vol. **115** Racial Discrimination
Vol. **116** Grief and Loss
Vol. **117** Self-Esteem and Body Image
Vol. **118** Focus on Sport
Vol. **119** Transport Trends
Vol. **120** The Human Rights Issue
Vol. **121** The Censorship Debate

Vol. **122** Bullying
Vol. **123** Young People and Health
Vol. **124** Parenting Issues
Vol. **125** Understanding Depression
Vol. **126** The Abortion Debate
Vol. **127** Eating Disorders
Vol. **128** The Cannabis Issue
Vol. **129** Gambling Trends
Vol. **130** Homelessness
Vol. **131** Citizenship and National Identity
Vol. **132** Child Abuse
Vol. **133** Teen Pregnancy and Lone Parents
Vol. **134** Customers and Consumerism
Vol. **135** Coping with Disability
Vol. **136** Self-Harm
Vol. **137** Crime and Anti-Social Behaviour
Vol. **138** A Genetically Modified Future?
Vol. **139** The Education Problem
Vol. **140** Vegetarian and Vegan Diets
Vol. **141** Mental Health
Vol. **142** Media Issues
Vol. **143** Problem Drinking

Vol. **144** The Cloning Debate
Vol. **145** Smoking Trends
Vol. **146** Sustainability and Environment
Vol. **147** The Terrorism Problem
Vol. **148** Religious Beliefs
Vol. **149** A Classless Society?
Vol. **150** Migration and Population
Vol. **151** Climate Change
Vol. **152** Euthanasia and the Right to Die
Vol. **153** Sexual Orientation and Society
Vol. **154** The Gender Gap
Vol. **155** Domestic Abuse
Vol. **156** Travel and Tourism
Vol. **157** The Problem of Globalisation
Vol. **158** The Internet Revolution
Vol. **159** An Ageing Population
Vol. **160** Poverty and Exclusion
Vol. **161** Waste Issues
Vol. **162** Staying Fit
Vol. **163** Drugs in the UK

dignity *see* human dignity
dinosaurs, extinction of **78**.1
direct debit **74**.9, 19, 24
direct discrimination **153**.37-8
direct mail scams **134**.26-8
direct racial discrimination **115**.7, 11
disability
    benefits **135**.3, 4, 5-6
    costs of **135**.5, 17, 18
    definition **135**.2
    discrimination **135**.1, 3, 28-9
      workplace **135**.15
    and employment **107**.12; **135**.3, 4, 14, 15
    and the media **135**.29, 32, 35
    and poverty **135**.16, 17-18; **160**.10, 25
    public attitudes to **135**.1, 30-31
    UK statistics **135**.1, 2-3, 6
    worldwide statistics **135**.25
Disability Agenda, DRC **135**.16, 31
Disability Discrimination Act **135**.13, 22, 31
    and schools **135**.38-9
    and workplace stress **100**.17, 20, 22
disability rights, UN treaty **135**.26
disability symbol **135**.14
disabled babies
    and abortion **126**.9, 34, 35
disabled children **107**.21
    choice in education **135**.24-5
    in developing countries **135**.26
    resources for **135**.21
    and sexual development **132**.29
    violence against **135**.27
disabled people
    and assisted suicide **152**.20-21
    discrimination **135**.1, 3
    and employment **107**.12; **135**.3, 4, 14, 15
    and football **118**.22
    and transport **135**.7-9
disabled person's railcard **135**.8
disablism **135**.28-9
disaster victims, older people **159**.6
discipline
    approaches to **132**.18
    parental **124**.2
    in schools, problems **120**.16
discrimination
    and child labour **99**.4
    direct and indirect **115**.7, 11
    disabled people **135**.1, 3, 15, 28-9
    against middle class university applications **149**.7
    and obesity **162**.21
    racial *see* racial discrimination
    refugee children **120**.22
    sexual orientation **153**.2-3
      in employment **153**.37-8
    by social class **149**.2
    in the workplace **135**.15; **153**.37-8
disease
    and medical research **103**.12-13, 16
    Millennium Development Goals **160**.32
    water-related **76**.2, 3, 5, 6, 9, 12, 19, 20, 35; **146**.14, 15

and children **76**.2, 3, 5, 9, 13
displaced persons **89**.1, 6, 8-9
disposable nappies, waste **161**.1, 5, 29
disruptive behaviour disorder, influence of media violence
    121.35
dissociative disorders **141**.11-13
distraction techniques, self-harmers **136**.5, 16, 19, 21
diuretics **118**.35, 37
diversity
    Britain **156**.11
    as business benefit **135**.14
    and sport **118**.12
divorce **106**.27-39
    and children **124**.29-30, 32, 33-4
    and male depression **125**.14
DIY abortions **126**.32-4
DIY burials **116**.38-9
DNA **138**.4, 12; **144**.17
doctors
    and abortion **126**.12, 13, 24
    and bereavement support **116**.2
    and complementary medicine**81**.4
    and disability support **135**.4
    and euthanasia **152**.7, 8, 24-6, 27-8
    fears of rise in gambling **129**.31
    and help for eating disorders **127**.28
    and reporting a death **116**.31
doctrine of double effect **152**.1, 3, 5
Dolly the sheep **144**.1, 15, 30-31, 32, 34, 39
domestic abuse **124**.18; **137**.8; **155**.1-39
    in childhood, and low self-esteem **117**.32
    convictions **155**.36-7
    definitions **155**.1, 27
    help for perpetrators **155**.33-4
    helplines **133**.37; **155**.28-9
    and housing support **130**.30
    impact on children **155**.1, 4, 5, 19-25
    injuries sustained **155**.30
    leaving home **155**.4-5, 6-712-13, 27-8
    legal protection **155**.28
    and low self-esteem **117**.32
    male victims **155**.12-13
    myths and stereotypes **155**.3-5
    personal stories **155**.8-10, 22-4
    prevalence of **154**.12; **155**.5,10
    register of offenders **155**.39
    reluctance to seek help **155**.3-4, 5, 6, 7, 30-31
    same-sex relationships **155**.13-15
    seeking help **155**.3-4, 7, 30-31
    signs of abuse **155**.1-2
    statistics **155**.24-5
    support for victims **155**.6-7, 28-9
    tackling abuse **155**.27-39
    and young people **155**.21, 26
domestic appliances, household ownership **134**.3-4, 5
domestic waste *see* household waste
domestic workers
    children as **99**.1, 4, 7-10
    migrant workers **150**.15
donor insemination and parental rights **153**.34
doomsday tourism **156**.27

doorstep selling and consumer rights **134**.20
dopamine **141**.9
doping *see* drugs in sport
Down's syndrome
    and Alzheimer's disease **141**.7
    and learning disabilities **135**.33
downers *see* depressant drugs
downloading **158**.35-6
dress code
    Christianty **148**.2
    Hinduism **148**.3
    Islam **148**.4
    Judaism **148**.4
    Sikhism **148**.5
drink-driving **119**.8-9; **143**.23-4
    alcohol limit **143**.3, 4
driver behaviour **119**.7-9
driving
    and alcohol *see* drink-driving
    and cannabis use **128**.14
    and disabled people **135**.4, 7
    and mobile phones **158**.12
Drop the Debt protests **121**.14
drug abuse **128**.11; **163**.1, 3, 7
    costs **163**.21
    deaths from **163**.11-12
    declining **163**.22
    frequency **163**.3
    and HIV **96**.14, 26
    and homeless people **130**.11, 20
    parents' worries about **124**.17
    statistics **163**.3, 7, 24, 32
    worldwide **163**.25
    young people **163**.3, 15-16, 18-19, 26-30
drug addiction **163**.2
drug development
    and animal experiments **103**.2-3, 9, 10, 11, 13
    use of stem cells **144**.18
drug misuse **163**.1
drug overdoses **163**.12
    first aid **136**.23
    statistics **136**.26

drug testing **118**.25
    statistics **118**.33-4
    UK **118**.28, 30
    at work **128**.20
    World Anti-Doping Code **118**.31-2
drug treatments
    for depression **125**.7, 22, 32, 35
        manic depression **125**.19
    for gambling **129**.39
drugs
    and alcohol **143**.3, 10
    classification **163**.2, 31, 33-4, 37
        cannabis **163**.32, 35-6
        criticism of **163**.32
    and crime **163**.2-3, 23, 38
    definitions **163**.1, 31
    and dependency **141**.9
    depression caused by **125**.5-6, 10
    effects **123**.8, 14
        amphetamines **163**.4-5
        cannabis **163**.6, 9, 35-6
        cocaine **163**.4
        ecstasy **163**.5, 9-10
        ketamine **163**.19-20
        LSD **163**.6
        magic mushrooms **163**.6
        opiates **163**.5
        solvents **163**.6
    getting help **123**.14
    and the law **163**.1-2, 31-9
    and persistent offenders **137**.15
    and politics **163**.31-2
    risks **143**.21-2
    smuggling **163**.37-8
    support for families of drug users **163**.24
    types **163**.2
    for weight loss **162**.2-3, 6, 20
    and young people **123**.1-2, 8, 9, 14; **163**.3, 9, 15-16; 18-19;
        26-30
drugs in sport **118**.23-39
    anabolic steroids **118**.35, 36
    androstenedione **118**.35

Volume numbers appear first (in bold) followed by page numbers; a change in volume number is preceded by a semi-colon.

Vol. **74** Money Matters
Vol. **76** The Water Crisis
Vol. **78** Threatened Species
Vol. **81** Alternative Therapies
Vol. **82** Protecting our Privacy
Vol. **85** The Housing Crisis
Vol. **88** Food and Nutrition
Vol. **89** Refugees
Vol. **96** Preventing Sexual Diseases
Vol. **97** Energy Matters
Vol. **99** Exploited Children
Vol. **100** Stress and Anxiety
Vol. **103** Animal Rights
Vol. **106** Trends in Marriage
Vol. **107** Work Issues
Vol. **115** Racial Discrimination
Vol. **116** Grief and Loss
Vol. **117** Self-Esteem and Body Image
Vol. **118** Focus on Sport
Vol. **119** Transport Trends
Vol. **120** The Human Rights Issue
Vol. **121** The Censorship Debate

Vol. **122** Bullying
Vol. **123** Young People and Health
Vol. **124** Parenting Issues
Vol. **125** Understanding Depression
Vol. **126** The Abortion Debate
Vol. **127** Eating Disorders
Vol. **128** The Cannabis Issue
Vol. **129** Gambling Trends
Vol. **130** Homelessness
Vol. **131** Citizenship and National Identity
Vol. **132** Child Abuse
Vol. **133** Teen Pregnancy and Lone Parents
Vol. **134** Customers and Consumerism
Vol. **135** Coping with Disability
Vol. **136** Self-Harm
Vol. **137** Crime and Anti-Social Behaviour
Vol. **138** A Genetically Modified Future?
Vol. **139** The Education Problem
Vol. **140** Vegetarian and Vegan Diets
Vol. **141** Mental Health
Vol. **142** Media Issues
Vol. **143** Problem Drinking

Vol. **144** The Cloning Debate
Vol. **145** Smoking Trends
Vol. **146** Sustainability and Environment
Vol. **147** The Terrorism Problem
Vol. **148** Religious Beliefs
Vol. **149** A Classless Society?
Vol. **150** Migration and Population
Vol. **151** Climate Change
Vol. **152** Euthanasia and the Right to Die
Vol. **153** Sexual Orientation and Society
Vol. **154** The Gender Gap
Vol. **155** Domestic Abuse
Vol. **156** Travel and Tourism
Vol. **157** The Problem of Globalisation
Vol. **158** The Internet Revolution
Vol. **159** An Ageing Population
Vol. **160** Poverty and Exclusion
Vol. **161** Waste Issues
Vol. **162** Staying Fit
Vol. **163** Drugs in the UK

athletes' responsibilities 118.32-3
beta-blockers 118.37
caffeine 118.35
cannabinoids 118.38
clenbuterol 118.35
consequences of abuse 118.32, 24
diuretics 118.35, 37
effects of drugs 118.35-8
ephedrine 118.35
erythropoetin 118.35
history of 118.23-5
hormones 118.37
medication and banned substances 118.32-3
nadrolone precursors 118.35
nalbuphine 118.35
narcotic analgesics 118.38
peptide hormones and analogues 118.37
pressure to take drugs 118.28-9
stimulants 118.36-7
duty solicitors 137.36

E

e-learning 139.28
e-mail
bullying 122.5, 19, 21
phishing 134.27-8, 28-9
security measures 134.28
spam 82.31-3, 36-7
surveillance of
and the Government 82.1, 22, 23
in the workplace 82.25, 26, 27, 28, 30; 120.32
E-number food additives and vegetarianism 140.18
e-university 139.28
early medical abortion (EMA) 14, 33
earnings
effect of education 139.1
gender gap see gender pay gap
graduates 139.35, 36, 37
and social class 149.2
minimum wage 107.31
teachers 139.12
ears, stem cell therapy 144.22
eating disorders 117.17-18; 123.7, 33-4; 127.1-31
binge eating 117.2, 15-16
and body image 117.27
causes 117.2-3, 6-7
children 117.3, 20-21
and compulsive exercise 162.39
health risks 117.4-5
prevention programmes 117.15, 18
signs and symptoms 117.2, 3, 17-19
anorexia 117.1, 2
binge eating 117.15, 16
body dysmorphic disorder 117.18-19
bulimia 117.1-2, 13, 14
support for sufferers 117.25-6, 28-30
treatment 117.28-9
binge eating 117.16
bulimia 117.14

obesity 117.34
eating habits see diet; healthy eating
eco-lodges 156.24
ecological debt 146.4-6; 150.32
ecological footprints 146.10, 17
ecological overshoot 146.10
economic globalisation 157.2
economic growth
Britain 134.24
costs of 157.13
and globalisation 157.36-7
impact of educational underachievement 149.39
impact of immigration 150.11, 17
economic hardship following divorce, effect on children 124.34
economic migrants and homelessness 130.19
economy
and refugees 89.21, 22, 30-1
and tobacco 145.22-3
ecosystems
biodiversity 146.18,19
and climate change 151.9
degradation of freshwater 76.35
and water consumption 76.2, 16-17, 19
ecotourism 156.20, 24
eco-towns 151.32
eco-travel spending 134.32
ecstasy (MDMA) 163.5, 9-10
deaths fron 163.11
and depression 125.10
risks 143.22
safety 163.34
street sales 163.12-13
use, Europe 163.25
ECT (electro-convulsive therapy) 125.25-6, 34, 35
ectomorph body shape 127.22
education 139.1-39
and alcohol 143.20
and behaviour problems in schools 120.16
body image improvement programmes 117.15
and black history 115.16-17
and black pupils 115.19-21
effects of cannabis use 128.14
and child labour 99.3, 7, 15; 120.18-19
and child soldiers 99.31
and children's rights 120.11
costs 124.3; 139.1; 160.16-17
and disabled children 135.24-5, 26; 36-9
on drugs 163.24
and earnings 139.1, 35, 36, 37
and ethnicity 139.8-9
faith-based schools 148.34, 35-6
and family income 149.25
and gender 139.10-11; 154.12, 22-7
global gender inequality 154.12
higher education 139.29-39
home learning 139.27-8
and homeless people
level of education 130.15
needs 130.34-5
on intelligent design 148.39
and learning disabilities 135.36-9

in mental health **141**.37
Millennium Development Goals **160**.30-31
and minority ethnic pupils **115**.18
in money matters **74**.1, 5-6, 12, 13
multi-faith schools **148**.32-3
and parents' mental health problems **141**.24
PE **118**.3
personal, social and health education **133**.16
and poverty **160**.2, 17-22
and racial integration **115**.29, 30, 37
and racism **115**.19-20
about sexual abuse **132**.27
about sexually transmitted infections **123**.25
and smoking **145**.3
and social mobility **139**.13; **149**.22, 25, 30, 36-7
special educational needs (SEN) **135**.36-9
statistics **139**.1-2
and teenage mothers **133**.24
underachievement, costs of **149**.39
and war-affected children **99**.34
and young people with HIV/AIDS **96**.26, 32, 33
young people's attitudes to **123**.2
and youth crime **137**.13
educational achievement
black pupils **115**.20
and ethnicity **139**.8
and family income **149**.25
gender differences **154**.22, 23
effect of poverty **160**.2, 18-19, 20, 21
and school pupil intake **149**.31-3
and single-sex schooling **139**.11-12
and social class **149**.30, 31-3
eggs
consumer choices **140**.37-8
free-range **140**.6, 29, 38-9
from GM hens, and cancer treatment **138**.20-21
and health **140**.30, 39
production methods **140**.29, 38-9
sales **140**.37-8
and vegetarian diets **140**.6, 19, 26
elderly people
and dementia *see* dementia

and depression **125**.22-3
elder abuse **159**.4, 6, 16-18
and homelessness **130**.17-18
and housing **85**.2, 10, 15
and mental health problems **141**.2
elections **131**.16-22
campaigns **131**.18
European **131**.15
General Elections **131**.18
terminology **131**.17
voter turnout **131**.19-21
electoral register **131**.16
electoral system **131**.15-26
electric hybrid vehicles **119**.22
electric vehicles **119**.21-2
electro-convulsive therapy (ECT) **125**.25-6, 34, 35
electronic equipment recycling **161**.8-9, 23-4
electronic footprints **158**.10-11
elephants
ivory trade **78**.20
killing of **78**.4, 6, 19
ELVs, recycling **161**.23
embarkation controls **150**.7
embryo cloning *see* human reproductive cloning
embryo donors **144**.7
embryonic stem cell research **144**.2
ethical issues **144**.6
humanist view **144**.7-8
embryos, hybrid **144**.9, 11, 14, 20
emergency contraception (EC) **126**.24
emergency treatment
for alcohol overdose **123**.16
self-harmers **136**.22-3
emigrants
British **150**.24-5
definition **150**.21
emissions
calculations **151**.22
reduction **151**.2, 13, 17, 36-7
transport **119**.1, 15, 31
aircraft **119**.16
and climate change **119**.14, 24, 30

Volume numbers appear first (in bold) followed by page numbers; a change in volume number is preceded by a semi-colon.

Vol. 74 Money Matters
Vol. 76 The Water Crisis
Vol. 78 Threatened Species
Vol. 81 Alternative Therapies
Vol. 82 Protecting our Privacy
Vol. 85 The Housing Crisis
Vol. 88 Food and Nutrition
Vol. 89 Refugees
Vol. 96 Preventing Sexual Diseases
Vol. 97 Energy Matters
Vol. 99 Exploited Children
Vol. 100 Stress and Anxiety
Vol. 103 Animal Rights
Vol. 106 Trends in Marriage
Vol. 107 Work Issues
Vol. 115 Racial Discrimination
Vol. 116 Grief and Loss
Vol. 117 Self-Esteem and Body Image
Vol. 118 Focus on Sport
Vol. 119 Transport Trends
Vol. 120 The Human Rights Issue
Vol. 121 The Censorship Debate

Vol. 122 Bullying
Vol. 123 Young People and Health
Vol. 124 Parenting Issues
Vol. 125 Understanding Depression
Vol. 126 The Abortion Debate
Vol. 127 Eating Disorders
Vol. 128 The Cannabis Issue
Vol. 129 Gambling Trends
Vol. 130 Homelessness
Vol. 131 Citizenship and National Identity
Vol. 132 Child Abuse
Vol. 133 Teen Pregnancy and Lone Parents
Vol. 134 Customers and Consumerism
Vol. 135 Coping with Disability
Vol. 136 Self-Harm
Vol. 137 Crime and Anti-Social Behaviour
Vol. 138 A Genetically Modified Future?
Vol. 139 The Education Problem
Vol. 140 Vegetarian and Vegan Diets
Vol. 141 Mental Health
Vol. 142 Media Issues
Vol. 143 Problem Drinking

Vol. 144 The Cloning Debate
Vol. 145 Smoking Trends
Vol. 146 Sustainability and Environment
Vol. 147 The Terrorism Problem
Vol. 148 Religious Beliefs
Vol. 149 A Classless Society?
Vol. 150 Migration and Population
Vol. 151 Climate Change
Vol. 152 Euthanasia and the Right to Die
Vol. 153 Sexual Orientation and Society
Vol. 154 The Gender Gap
Vol. 155 Domestic Abuse
Vol. 156 Travel and Tourism
Vol. 157 The Problem of Globalisation
Vol. 158 The Internet Revolution
Vol. 159 An Ageing Population
Vol. 160 Poverty and Exclusion
Vol. 161 Waste Issues
Vol. 162 Staying Fit
Vol. 163 Drugs in the UK

emotional abuse **132**.1, 5-6; **155**.3
   signs of **132**.4-5
emotional blackmail by parents **124**.15
emotional changes, and stress **100**.33
emotional damage caused by corporal punishment **132**.10, 19
emotional disorders, young people **125**.9
emotional distress as cause of eating disorders **127**.2
emotional health problems of consumerism **134**.5
emotional impact of domestic violence **155**.30
emotional literacy classes **141**.37
emotional neglect in childhood, and low self-esteem **117**.32
emotional problems, sharing **123**.10
emotions, animals **140**.27-8
employees, gambling at work **129**.22-4
employers
   basic skills requirements **139**.17
   equality policies **115**.13
   liability for racism **115**.12
   links with higher education **139**.38-9
   and privacy rights in the workplace **82**.25-30
   and workplace stress **100**.17-18, 20
employment
   and age discrimination **159**.8-13
   barriers to **160**.13
   census information **150**.36
   of disabled people **107**.12; **135**.3, 4, 14, 15
   effect of free trade **157**.13, 23
   and gender **154**.29-35
   effect of globalisation **157**.36-7
   graduates **139**.33
   and homeless people **130**.15, 36-7
   inequalities **149**.28
   and lone parents **133**.28
   and mental illness **141**.22
   effect of migration **150**.9-10
   and obesity discrimination **162**.21
   from recycling **161**.2
   past retirement age **159**.10, 15
   and racism **115**.12, 13
   sexual orientation discrimination **153**.37-9
   students **74**.20, 29, 37; **139**.35
   tourism industry **156**.10
   working conditions, international companies **157**.11
employment of refugees **89**.22-3, 24, 26-7, 32
   illegal employment of refugees **89**.10-11, 30-1
empty houses
   and environmental decline **85**.14
   numbers of **85**.25, 29
   and the vacancy rate **85**.9, 25
endangered species **78**.1-3
   birds **78**.2, 8-9, 27, 29, 37
   and the killing of wildlife **78**.2, 4-5, 5-6
   mammals **78**.3, 27, 28, 32
   plants **78**.2-3, 7, 17, 21, 36
   and pollution **78**.6
   trade in **78**.16-17, 19-22, 38-9
   in the UK **78**.28-31
endocrine disorders and depression **125**.5
endogenous (unipolar) depression **125**.4, 10
endomorph body shape **127**.22
energy

and the countryside **97**.24-5
   and exercise **141**.39
   household costs and poverty **160**.22-3
   and meat-eating **140**.21
   and nutrition, teenagers **123**.6-7
   output of the energy industry **97**.3
   production and supply **97**.3-4
   public attitudes to energy and environment **97**.34-6
   saving through recycling **161**.22
   from waste **161**.20, 38, 39
energy consumption **97**.6
   construction industry **146**.11
   increasing **146**.39
energy dependence of UK **146**.5-6
energy efficiency **97**.27-33; **151**.29
   and global warming **97**.29
   in the home **97**.2, 27-30, 31, 32-3; **151**.39
   and renewable energy sources **97**.11
   and shopping **97**.31-2
   and sustainable housing **85**.37
   and transport **97**.24, 25, 31
English language, diversification **157**.16
entertainment and the Internet **158**.3, 7, 21-2
entrepreneurs **107**.4
environment
   and agriculture **146**.25
   and air travel **156**.21, 26
   effects of genetic modification **138**.12-14, 24
   effect of globalisation **157**.10
   and housing **85**.14-15, 26
   information requests **142**.19
   and meat production **140**.13, 16-7
   effect of migration **150**.26-7
   protection of **88**.32, 34, 35
   public attitudes to **97**.34
   and self-esteem **117**.37, 38-9
   and tobacco **145**.23
   impact of tourism **156**.20, 21, 22, 25
      air travel **156**.21, 26
      reducing **156**.24
   and transnational companies **157**.10-11
   and urban growth **146**.17
   and water bills **76**.33, 34
   and World Trade Organisation **157**.22-3
environmental globalisation **157**.2
environmental migration **146**.16-17
environmental sustainability *see* sustainability
environmental taxes **157**.12-13
environmental tobacco smoke *see* passive smoking
environmentally cleaner vehicles **119**.20-23
ephedrine **118**.35
epidemiology (population studies) **103**.17, 18, 19, 22
epilepsy and learning disabilities **135**.34
equal opportunity in sport **118**.12-13, 15-16, 18-19, 22
equal pay *see* gender pay gap
equality rights, disabled people **135**.13
equity in sport **118**.12
   gender equity **118**.18-19
erythropoetin (EPO) **118**.35, 37
escalation theory of drug use **128**.9-10, 11, 28
escharotics (cancer salves) **81**.33

established church 148.21-2
estimates and consumer rights 134.18
ethical consumerism 134.30-38
ethical crime, Europe 137.6
ethical food 134.32, 34-7
ethical trade 134.36; 157.18
ethical travel 134.30
ethics
    of genetic modification 138.23
    of human cloning 144.2-3, 5-6, 7-8
ethnic groups interaction 147.19
ethnic minorities
    British identity 115.38
    and community feelings 131.2
    and country of birth 131.8
    and education 115.18; 139.8-9
    and football 118.13-16
    and identity cards 82.2, 8
    interest in the news 142.32-3
    and mental illness 141.23
    mixed race population in the UK 115.24-5
    and national identity 131.1, 8
    and racial discrimination perception 131.2-3
    social mobility 149.21-2
    and the UK census 115.3
    as victims of crime 115.10
ethnic origin
    and age of population, UK 150.39
    and body image 117.29-30
    census data 150.36
    and education 139.8-9
    gender and educational achievement 154.23
    gender and pupil behaviour 154.24
    as grounds for discrimination 115.7
    homeless people 130.10, 14
    and poverty 160.2
    women in the workforce 154.29
    young people and sex 123.19-20
ethnic stereotypes and reality TV shows 115.22
Europe
    alcohol trends 143.21, 31
    cannabis use 128.21-2

online gambling 129.20
European Court of Human Rights 153.31
    and gay adoption 153.31
    and parental rights 153.34
European Union
    accession countries, migration from 150.6-7
    ban on advertising tobacco 145.7
    and biotechnology 138.28-9
    carbon credits 151.35, 37
    citizenship 131.38
    elections 131.15
    GM ban, effect on developing countries 138.29-30
    and ID cards 131.13
    smoking 145.21
    students from EU countries 139.30, 32
    views of young people 131.39
    and wildlife trade 146.34
    workplace gender gap 154.17-18, 33
euthanasia 152.1-39
    active 152.5
    arguments against 152.3-4, 5, 17-18
    arguments for 152.3-4, 6, 10
    and treatment of babies 152.4, 32, 33, 34
    definitions 152.1, 2, 5, 19
    diminishing respect for life 152.3-4
    involuntary 152.1
    law on 152.1, 16-18, 29-30
    medical profession's attitudes 152.7, 8, 24-6, 27-8
    non-voluntary 152.1, 3
    in other countries 152.4, 18, 19, 31, 33
    and religious faith 152.7, 12, 15
        Church of England 152.34
        Roman Catholic Church 152.3-4
    statistics 152.17, 23, 24, 25
evidence obtained under torture 120.39
evolution
    and animals 78.1
    public opinions on 148.37
exams 139.4
    results
        A-levels 139.18
        academies 139.14, 15

Volume numbers appear first (in bold) followed by page numbers; a change in volume number is preceded by a semi-colon.

Vol. **74** Money Matters
Vol. **76** The Water Crisis
Vol. **78** Threatened Species
Vol. **81** Alternative Therapies
Vol. **82** Protecting our Privacy
Vol. **85** The Housing Crisis
Vol. **88** Food and Nutrition
Vol. **89** Refugees
Vol. **96** Preventing Sexual Diseases
Vol. **97** Energy Matters
Vol. **99** Exploited Children
Vol. **100** Stress and Anxiety
Vol. **103** Animal Rights
Vol. **106** Trends in Marriage
Vol. **107** Work Issues
Vol. **115** Racial Discrimination
Vol. **116** Grief and Loss
Vol. **117** Self-Esteem and Body Image
Vol. **118** Focus on Sport
Vol. **119** Transport Trends
Vol. **120** The Human Rights Issue
Vol. **121** The Censorship Debate

Vol. **122** Bullying
Vol. **123** Young People and Health
Vol. **124** Parenting Issues
Vol. **125** Understanding Depression
Vol. **126** The Abortion Debate
Vol. **127** Eating Disorders
Vol. **128** The Cannabis Issue
Vol. **129** Gambling Trends
Vol. **130** Homelessness
Vol. **131** Citizenship and National Identity
Vol. **132** Child Abuse
Vol. **133** Teen Pregnancy and Lone Parents
Vol. **134** Customers and Consumerism
Vol. **135** Coping with Disability
Vol. **136** Self-Harm
Vol. **137** Crime and Anti-Social Behaviour
Vol. **138** A Genetically Modified Future?
Vol. **139** The Education Problem
Vol. **140** Vegetarian and Vegan Diets
Vol. **141** Mental Health
Vol. **142** Media Issues
Vol. **143** Problem Drinking

Vol. **144** The Cloning Debate
Vol. **145** Smoking Trends
Vol. **146** Sustainability and Environment
Vol. **147** The Terrorism Problem
Vol. **148** Religious Beliefs
Vol. **149** A Classless Society?
Vol. **150** Migration and Population
Vol. **151** Climate Change
Vol. **152** Euthanasia and the Right to Die
Vol. **153** Sexual Orientation and Society
Vol. **154** The Gender Gap
Vol. **155** Domestic Abuse
Vol. **156** Travel and Tourism
Vol. **157** The Problem of Globalisation
Vol. **158** The Internet Revolution
Vol. **159** An Ageing Population
Vol. **160** Poverty and Exclusion
Vol. **161** Waste Issues
Vol. **162** Staying Fit
Vol. **163** Drugs in the UK

AS-levels **139**.18
 exceeding expectation **139**.22
 GCSEs **139**.2
 gender differences **154**.22, 23
  and single-sex schooling **139**.12; **154**.27
 standards **139**.19-20
 and stress **100**.3-7; **123**.29-30
  causes of **100**.5
  dealing with **100**.5, 6
  getting help and advice with **100**.3
exchange rate, effect on tourism **156**.1, 7-8
exclusion clauses and consumer rights **134**.19-20
exclusions from school
 black pupils **115**.19-20; **139**.9
 and ethnicity **139**.8, 9
 gender differences **154**.24
exercise **88**.1, 2-3, 11, 12, 18; **162**.6; 29-34
 and the ageing process **159**.33; **162**.12
 barriers to **162**.24, 29
 benefits of **118**.3
  for women **118**.20
 children **119**.31; **162**.6, 26, 28, 29
  effect on weight **162**.28, 29
  lack of exercise **162**.13, 15, 25
 compulsive **162**.39
 and depression **125**.3, 20, 39; **162**.37, 38
 and giving up smoking **145**.36
 government strategy **162**.18
 and health **162**.11-12, 29-31
 lack of *see* inactivity
 and life expectancy **159**.33
 and mental health **141**.34, 39; **162**.37, 38
 motivation for **162**.30-31
 and obesity **162**.28, 29, 36
 older people **159**.39
 recommended amounts **162**.30
 and self-esteem **117**.37, 38
 statistics **162**.6
 and stress
  benefits of **100**.19, 27, 30, 34, 36, 37
 and weight loss **162**.20
 when not to exercise **162**.31-2
 in the workplace **162**.23, 24
 and young people **123**.2, 7
exhaust gases *see* emissions, transport
exploitation of workers **120**.28-31
 migrant workers **150**.14, 15, 19, 20, 22
expression, freedom of *see* freedom of expression
extended schools **149**.30, 37-8
extended warranties **134**.19
external costs of motoring **119**.14
extra-curricular activities and social mobility **149**.30, 37-8
extremism
 monitoring extremist networks **147**.13-14
 tackling **147**.33-4; **148**.30-31
extremist parties **131**.23-4
 impact on democracy **131**.24
eyes
 stem cell therapy **144**.22
 test for Alzheimer's disease **141**.19

F

facial recognition technology **82**.3, 6, 17
 and identity cards **82**.9, 10
facial stem cell therapy **144**.21-2
factory farming and animal cloning **144**.35
fair trade **134**.34-7; **157**.18, 27, 31-4
 coffee **157**.32, 33
 cotton **157**.28, 34
 ineffectiveness **157**.34
Fairtrade mark **134**.35, 37
faith differences and relationships **115**.39
faith hate crime **115**.27
faith schools **148**.34, 35-6
falls, older people **159**.4, 6
False Memory Syndrome **132**.34-5
families
 abuse of older people **159**.17
 adjusting to a new family **124**.31
 and body image **117**.14
 and drinking behaviour of young people **143**.5, 17
 changing family patterns **106**.1-2; **124**.20-39
 and debt problems **74**.3, 5-6; **160**.12
 digital technology usage **158**.7-8
 and disability **135**.4
 of drug users, support for **163**.24
 equality issues **154**.3
 family conflict and street homelessness **130**.10
 and football **141**.33
 income, effect on educational attainment **149**.25
 of lesbians and gay people, support **153**.10
 low income, broadband access **158**.18
 and manic depressives **125**.20
 and mobile phones **158**.13
 and poverty **160**.13-14
 pressure on athletes to take drugs **118**.29
 problems **124**.18
  young people's worries **123**.3
 reaction to mixed-faith relationships **115**.39
 and relationship support **106**.29-30
 size
  influenced by costs of raising children **124**.18
 and working parents **124**.1, 21
family planning
 and teenagers **133**.2
farming *see* agriculture; organic farming
fashion, and the fur trade **103**.36-7
fashion industry, employment conditions **157**.27-9
fasting
 Christianity **148**.10
 Islam **148**.11
fat **162**.8
 spot-reduction **162**.33
fat intake **88**.2, 5, 7, 8
 and food labelling **88**.21-2, 22-3
 and red meat **140**.12
 teenagers **123**.7
fathers
 and abortion **126**.13, 15-16
 and childcare **124**.7-11

impact on children's achievement **124**.7
employment patterns **107**.24-5
full-time fathers **124**.9-10
and household tasks **124**.11
new fathers and depression **125**.14
paternity leave **107**.25
rights and responsibilities **133**.39
teenage fathers **133**.25-7
unmarried, and parental responsibility **124**.4
working fathers **107**.24-25
fatty acids
    and ADHD (attention-deficit hyperactivity disorder) **141**.19
    in diet **141**.30
fatwa **147**.15
faulty goods, consumer rights **134**.17
favouritism by parents **124**.15
fear of crime **137**.5, 7
fear of terrorism **147**.12
fear after traumatic bereavement **116**.11-12
fear of young people **137**.26-7
feelings
    of abuse victims **132**.22
    of animals **140**.27-8
    after bereavement **116**.1, 3-4, 5, 7-9, 10-11, 19, 21-2, 30
    healthy self-esteem **117**.30
    low self-esteem **117**.5
fees, university **139**.34
female condoms **123**.23
feminism and men **154**.7-8
fertility
    effect of abortion **126**.10
    effect of smoking **145**.32
    and environmental stress **146**.16-17
    UK **151**.32
    worldwide **150**.32-3, 34
fertility treatment, gay people **153**.33-4
festivals
    Buddhism **148**.2
    Christianity **148**.2
    Hinduism **148**.3
    Islam **148**.3
    Judaism **148**.4

Sikhism **148**.5
fetus
    abnormality and abortion **126**.9, 35
    development of **126**.26
    feeling pain **126**.22, 26
    rights **126**.21-2, 27
    viability **126**.27
fibre intake **88**.2, 5, 6, 23
filesharing **158**.36
films
    classification **121**.22, 23-5, 29-30
    cuts **121**.25
    online viewing **158**.21-2
    and smoking **145**.8-10
    violence, and playground bullying **121**.28
final warnings, criminal offences **137**.12
financial abuse and older people **159**.16
financial benefits *see* state benefits
financial disruption to terrorism **147**.3, 28
financial freedom, older people **159**.20
financial incentives
    for reducing waste **161**.38
    for weight loss **162**.22-3
financial planning for old age **159**.21-2
financial products, expenditure on **134**.4
financial support to adult children
    by grandmothers **124**.38
    by parents **124**.3
financial worries and non-traditional families **124**.20
fine particles, air pollution **146**.35
first aid **136**.22-3
    for drug emergencies **136**.23
fisheries **146**.28
fishing **103**.30
    and the protection of the oceans **78**.14
    and sustainability **146**.28-9
fitness
    effects on ageing **159**.33, 34; **162**.12
    equipment for older people **159**.39
    government strategy **162**.17-18
    inequalities **162**.35
    and mental health **141**.34, 39; **162**.37, 38

Volume numbers appear first (in bold) followed by page numbers; a change in volume number is preceded by a semi-colon.

Vol. **74** Money Matters
Vol. **76** The Water Crisis
Vol. **78** Threatened Species
Vol. **81** Alternative Therapies
Vol. **82** Protecting our Privacy
Vol. **85** The Housing Crisis
Vol. **88** Food and Nutrition
Vol. **89** Refugees
Vol. **96** Preventing Sexual Diseases
Vol. **97** Energy Matters
Vol. **99** Exploited Children
Vol. **100** Stress and Anxiety
Vol. **103** Animal Rights
Vol. **106** Trends in Marriage
Vol. **107** Work Issues
Vol. **115** Racial Discrimination
Vol. **116** Grief and Loss
Vol. **117** Self-Esteem and Body Image
Vol. **118** Focus on Sport
Vol. **119** Transport Trends
Vol. **120** The Human Rights Issue
Vol. **121** The Censorship Debate

Vol. **122** Bullying
Vol. **123** Young People and Health
Vol. **124** Parenting Issues
Vol. **125** Understanding Depression
Vol. **126** The Abortion Debate
Vol. **127** Eating Disorders
Vol. **128** The Cannabis Issue
Vol. **129** Gambling Trends
Vol. **130** Homelessness
Vol. **131** Citizenship and National Identity
Vol. **132** Child Abuse
Vol. **133** Teen Pregnancy and Lone Parents
Vol. **134** Customers and Consumerism
Vol. **135** Coping with Disability
Vol. **136** Self-Harm
Vol. **137** Crime and Anti-Social Behaviour
Vol. **138** A Genetically Modified Future?
Vol. **139** The Education Problem
Vol. **140** Vegetarian and Vegan Diets
Vol. **141** Mental Health
Vol. **142** Media Issues
Vol. **143** Problem Drinking

Vol. **144** The Cloning Debate
Vol. **145** Smoking Trends
Vol. **146** Sustainability and Environment
Vol. **147** The Terrorism Problem
Vol. **148** Religious Beliefs
Vol. **149** A Classless Society?
Vol. **150** Migration and Population
Vol. **151** Climate Change
Vol. **152** Euthanasia and the Right to Die
Vol. **153** Sexual Orientation and Society
Vol. **154** The Gender Gap
Vol. **155** Domestic Abuse
Vol. **156** Travel and Tourism
Vol. **157** The Problem of Globalisation
Vol. **158** The Internet Revolution
Vol. **159** An Ageing Population
Vol. **160** Poverty and Exclusion
Vol. **161** Waste Issues
Vol. **162** Staying Fit
Vol. **163** Drugs in the UK

motivation **162**.30-31

myths **162**.33-4

young people **123**.2

fitness industry, lack of effect on obesity **162**.35

flags **131**.3-4

flashbacks

about sexual abuse **132**.28

after violent crime **137**.9

flexible working **107**.2, 11-12, 14-19

father-friendly employment **107**.25

and lone parents **133**.38

right to request **107**.17-18, 21-2

flooding and climate change **151**.10-11

fly-tipping **161**.16

foetal alcohol spectrum disorder **143**.3, 33

foetal stem cells **144**.25

folate, increased in GM tomatoes **138**.14

food

and alcohol **143**.7

and animal cloning **144**.36-9

and energy efficiency **97**.32, 33

ethical **134**.34-7

food security **146**.12-13

food value of alcohol **143**.2

GM food *see* genetically modified (GM) crops

hunger *see* hunger

and mental health **141**.30-31, 34

organic **134**.31

production and global water supplies **76**.3, 4, 7, 18

and religion **148**.10-11

in schools, attitudes to **123**.32

supplies and GM crops **138**.9, 10, 34-5

UK dependence on imports **146**.5

and young people **123**.1

food advertising and children **134**.10

food labelling **88**.9, 21-5

GM food **138**.11, 39

food and nutrition **88**.1-39

additives **88**.13-14, 34, 36, 38, 39

advertising and promotion **88**.10, 11, 19, 20, 35, 37

food poisoning **88**.14, 27-9

food safety **88**.26, 32, 34

healthy diet **88**.1-2, 5-7

junk food **88**.9-11

locally grown produce **88**.31, 33

nutrition information panels **88**.21, 22-3

teenagers **123**.6-7

food packaging

recycling tins **161**.27

food poisoning **88**.14, 27-9

food production

and intensive farming **140**.36-7

and meat consumption **140**.13, 16-17

and mental health **141**.30

food security **157**.5

food waste **161**.4, 10-11, 19

foot-and-mouth disease

and the ban on hunting **103**.26

football

and disabled people **118**.22

and homophobia **118**.17

and mental health **141**.32-3

racial equality **118**.13-16

and violence **118**.7, 8

wages **118**.11

Football Association (FA)

anti-homophobia campaign **118**.17

and disabled supporters **118**.22

Football Foundation **118**.22

footwear for exercise **162**.32

forced labour **120**.28-30

children **120**.18-19

forced marriages **106**.15; **155**.16-18

foreign-born population

UK **150**.29, 30

worldwide **150**.33

foreign investment **157**.37

foreign students and terrorism **147**.13-14

forests

and carbon sequestration **151**.26

effect of increased trade **157**.14

and sustainability **146**.30-31

threatened species of animals in **78**.1, 2, 5

forgotten working poor **160**.22-3

fossil fuels

alternatives to reliance on **97**.2, 21

as an energy source **97**.8, 21

and biomass **97**.18

sustainable **151**.28-30

foster care, prohibition of corporal punishment **132**.15

fostering **133**.9

by gay people **153**.34

foundation schools **135**.36

foundation stage education, gender gap **154**.23

fraud

and identity cards **82**.2, 7, 8, 11, 12

phishing **134**.27-8, 28-9

scams **134**.26-8

free choice *see* autonomy

free newspapers **142**.9

free press **121**.1-2

free-range eggs **140**.6, 29

consumer choice **140**.37-8

and health **140**.30

production **140**.29, 38-9

free speech **121**.1-21

and the Internet **121**.18, 19; **158**.2

and law **121**.7

timeline **121**.3

free trade **157**.12-14, 17-18

benefits **157**.25

and developing countries **157**.20, 25, 26-7

effect on employment **157**.13, 23

effect on poverty **157**.9, 13

freedom of expression **121**.4

and cartoons of Mohammed **121**.10-13, 15-16; **142**.34

Freedom of Information Act **142**.18-20

delays in meeting requests **142**.20

and regional newspapers **142**.17

Freedom Food mark **140**.29, 34

fish **146**.29

freight transport trends **119**.1

frequent offenders **137**.11, 15, 16

freshers' flu **123**.4

friends

bullied, how to help **122**.13

with eating disorders, how to help **127**.30

as family **124**.19

manic depressives, how to help **125**.20

self-harmers, how to help **136**.16

fruit and vegetable consumption **162**.6

fruit machines **129**.2

and under 16s **129**.11

fruitarian diet **140**.2

fuel cell vehicles **119**.22-3

fuel efficient cars **119**.20-23

fuel poverty **160**.22-3

pensioners **159**.3

fuel taxes **119**.14, 24

aircraft **119**.16

fuels, cleaner **119**.20-23

full-time fathers **124**.9-10

full-time mothers, working hours **124**.12

fundamentalism, Islam **147**.15

funding

academies **139**.14

security services **147**.2

students **139**.34-5

funerals **116**.3, 16, 20, 33-5

alternative **116**.38-9

arranging **116**.32

children's questions about **116**.26

environmental **134**.31

and young people **116**.23

furnishings, spending on **134**.4

furniture recycling **161**.24

further education **139**.2

G7 and G8 countries **157**.5

G8 summit

climate change accord **151**.16-17

protests **121**.14

gambling **129**.1-39

addiction *see* compulsive gambling

addictiveness **129**.30

benefits **129**.18

controlled **129**.2, 28

definition **129**.1, 28

effects **129**.36

physical **129**.29, 36

psychological **129**.6, 29

research **129**.16

expenditure on **129**.4

children **129**.32, 33

mobile gambling **129**.26

National Lottery **129**.9, 10

online gambling **129**.17, 19

forms of **129**.2

Gambling Commission, The **129**.4-5

licence conditions **129**.8, 23

history of **129**.1

and law

Gambling Act **129**.5, 17, 23

and gambling at work **129**.23

online gambling **129**.17

licensing **129**.5, 8, 23

by mobiles **129**.18, 26

and neurobiology **129**.6

online gambling **129**.17-18, 19-25

participation in **129**.4

National Lottery **129**.9, 10

online gambling **129**.19

young people **129**.11

problem gamblers *see* compulsive gambling

psychology of **129**.6, 29

signs of problems **129**.22-3, 24, 28, 29, 35-6, 38

social factors **129**.7, 29

statistics **129**.1-3, 4

underage **129**.1

National Lottery **129**.11-13

online gambling **129**.18, 25

online poker **129**.25

Scotland **129**.32-3

Volume numbers appear first (in bold) followed by page numbers; a change in volume number is preceded by a semi-colon.

Vol. **74** Money Matters

Vol. **76** The Water Crisis

Vol. **78** Threatened Species

Vol. **81** Alternative Therapies

Vol. **82** Protecting our Privacy

Vol. **85** The Housing Crisis

Vol. **88** Food and Nutrition

Vol. **89** Refugees

Vol. **96** Preventing Sexual Diseases

Vol. **97** Energy Matters

Vol. **99** Exploited Children

Vol. **100** Stress and Anxiety

Vol. **103** Animal Rights

Vol. **106** Trends in Marriage

Vol. **107** Work Issues

Vol. **115** Racial Discrimination

Vol. **116** Grief and Loss

Vol. **117** Self-Esteem and Body Image

Vol. **118** Focus on Sport

Vol. **119** Transport Trends

Vol. **120** The Human Rights Issue

Vol. **121** The Censorship Debate

Vol. **122** Bullying

Vol. **123** Young People and Health

Vol. **124** Parenting Issues

Vol. **125** Understanding Depression

Vol. **126** The Abortion Debate

Vol. **127** Eating Disorders

Vol. **128** The Cannabis Issue

Vol. **129** Gambling Trends

Vol. **130** Homelessness

Vol. **131** Citizenship and National Identity

Vol. **132** Child Abuse

Vol. **133** Teen Pregnancy and Lone Parents

Vol. **134** Customers and Consumerism

Vol. **135** Coping with Disability

Vol. **136** Self-Harm

Vol. **137** Crime and Anti-Social Behaviour

Vol. **138** A Genetically Modified Future?

Vol. **139** The Education Problem

Vol. **140** Vegetarian and Vegan Diets

Vol. **141** Mental Health

Vol. **142** Media Issues

Vol. **143** Problem Drinking

Vol. **144** The Cloning Debate

Vol. **145** Smoking Trends

Vol. **146** Sustainability and Environment

Vol. **147** The Terrorism Problem

Vol. **148** Religious Beliefs

Vol. **149** A Classless Society?

Vol. **150** Migration and Population

Vol. **151** Climate Change

Vol. **152** Euthanasia and the Right to Die

Vol. **153** Sexual Orientation and Society

Vol. **154** The Gender Gap

Vol. **155** Domestic Abuse

Vol. **156** Travel and Tourism

Vol. **157** The Problem of Globalisation

Vol. **158** The Internet Revolution

Vol. **159** An Ageing Population

Vol. **160** Poverty and Exclusion

Vol. **161** Waste Issues

Vol. **162** Staying Fit

Vol. **163** Drugs in the UK

at work **129**.22-4
women **129**.21, 27, 34
young people **129**.1
   addiction **129**.25, 31, 32-3
   National Lottery **129**.11-13
   signs of gambling problems **129**.38
   views on gambling **129**.13
gaming
   addiction to **158**.39
   concerns about violence **158**.33
gangs and teenage safety **137**.20
gap years **107**.27; **156**.15-19
gardens and water conservation **76**.1, 36, 37, 38
garment companies, working conditions **157**.27-9
gastric surgery for weight loss **162**.3
gateway effect, cannabis use **128**.9-10, 11, 28
GATS (General Agreement on Trade and Services) **157**.6
GATT (General Agreement on Trade and Tariffs) **157**.5-6
gay adoption **153**.31-2
gay couples
   adoption and fostering **153**.34
   fertility treatment **153**.33-4
   having a child **153**.20-22
gay gene theory **153**.6
gay issues in children's literature **153**.19-20
gay men
   in boardroom positions **153**.39
   and depression **125**.15
   and HIV **96**.17, 20, 23
   and the media **142**.39
   and sexually transmitted infections (STIs) **96**.3, 4, 10, 12
GCSEs **139**.4
   academies **139**.14, 15
   and ethnicity **139**.8
   gender differences **154**.22
   results **139**.2
GDP (Gross Domestic Product) **157**.6
   as measure of living standards **157**.13
geep (sheep-goat chimera) 10
gender
   and alcohol consumption **143**.16, 31
   and alcohol effects **143**.7
   and alcohol limits **143**.27
   and Alzheimer's disease **159**.36
   and bullying **122**.18
   and cannabis use **128**.22
   and car use **119**.29
   and child pedestrian accidents **119**.5
   of children and effects of divorce **124**.33
   and compulsive shopping **134**.14
   definition **154**.1
   and depression **125**.2
   development **154**.1
   differences **154**.1, 9
   and disability **135**.2
   and drug abuse **163**.29-30
   and education see gender and education
   homeless people **130**.10, 14
   and mental ill-health **141**.1
   and online shopping **134**.16
   and pay see gender pay gap

and schizophrenia **141**.4
and self-harm **136**.7, 24, 26
and smoking **145**.1, 21, 22
   children **145**.2, 5
and society **154**.1-14
and stress **100**.13, 19
and suicide risk **136**.33
victims of crime **137**.4, 7
and work **154**.29-35
young people in custody **137**.15
youth offenders **137**.14, 16
gender-based violence **154**.12
gender and education **139**.10-11; **154**.22-7
   A-level performance **139**.18
   and educational performance **139**.2; **154**.22, 23
   higher education **139**.32
   reasons for gender gap **154**.25
   subject choices **139**.11; **154**.26
   worldwide **154**.12
gender equality
   changes since 1970s **154**.5
   Gender Equality Duty **154**.5
   goals **154**.2-4, 6
   Millennium Development Goals **160**.13
   and Oxfam programmes **154**.12
gender equity in sport **118**.18-19
gender inequality **154**.2-4
   worldwide **154**.12-14
gender pay gap **107**.13, 25, 26; **154**.2-3, 6, 30, 35-9
   graduates **139**.36
   senior management **154**.38
gender power gap **154**.4, 6
gender-specific behaviour **154**.1, 9
gender stereotypes
   in careers advice **154**.28
   male **154**.7-8
gender and work **154**.29-35
   careers advice **154**.28, 35
   and pay see gender pay gap
General Agreement on Trade and Services (GATS) **157**.6
General Agreement on Trade and Tariffs (GATT) **157**.5-6
gene doping **118**.34
gene splicing see genetic modification
gene therapy **118**.39
General Elections **131**.18
genes **138**.4, 12
   and addiction **141**.9
   and ageing **159**.2, 32
   and Alzheimer's disease **159**.36
   and attention-deficit hyperactivity disorder (ADHD) **141**.19
   and depression **125**.2
   and eating disorders **127**.6-7
   and obesity **127**.35; **162**.9-10
   and sexuality **153**.6, 7
genetic barriers **144**.12
genetic biodiversity **146**.18
genetic engineering **144**.20
genetic modification
   definition **138**.1, 2, 4
   and the environment **138**.12-14, 24
   ethical issues **138**.23

limitations **138**.37-8
product labeling **138**.11, 25, 39
public attitudes to **138**.3, 15-16
technologies **138**.35
Genetic Use Restriction Technologies (GURTs) **138**.18
genetically modified animals, experiments on **103**.1, 8, **144**.34
genetically modified (GM) crops **88**.14, 32, 33; **146**.26-7
and animal feed **138**.25
benefits of **138**.8-10
crop area **138**.2, 25, 29
cross-contamination **138**.6-7, 12-13
developing countries **138**.9, 10, 23, 29-30, 34-5
drug crops (pharming) **138**.4, 9-10, 20-22
and food production **140**.37
future for **138**.13; **146**.26-7
land register proposal **138**.36
non-food crops **138**.10, 14
potato research trials **138**.27, 28
rice **138**.20, 31-4
risks **138**.8-10, 24
safety **138**.6
tobacco plants **138**.21-2
UK **138**.2-3, 5, 39
genetically modified organisms (GMOs)
benefits **138**.12
concerns about **138**.12-13, 24
definition **138**.4, 12
hens **138**.20-21
genetics research **103**.11, 13
genital herpes **96**.3, 4
and HIV **96**.12
genital warts **96**.2-3, 4, 12-13
Genito-Urinary Medicine (GUM) clinics **96**.1, 10
health advisers and safer sex **96**.1, 10
and HIV testing **96**.16
pressure on services **96**.3, 4, 8-9, 11
and sexually transmitted infections **123**.25
tests and treatment offered at **96**.10
genomics **138**.2-3, 37-9
geospatial intelligence **120**.34
geothermal energy **97**.6-7, 9, 11-12
germ line therapy **144**.20

germ line transmission **144**.26
germs **88**.27, 28-9
ghettos **115**.28, 31
gifted and talented scheme, and black pupils **139**.9
girls' schools **154**.27
girls and young women
and body image **117**.14-15, 19, 20-21, 22, 25
and bullying **122**.10, 14, 15-16
careers information **154**.28, 35
and child labour **99**.2, 3
child soldiers **99**.29, 31, 36
and cosmetic surgery **117**.26-8
and dieting **117**.20-21
discrimination against **154**.13-14
drug abuse **163**.29-30
and education **154**.22-6
examination results **154**.22, 23
foundation stage **154**.23
single-sex education **154**.27
subject choices **154**.22, 26
and mental health problems **141**.1
and plastic surgery **117**.26-8
and puberty **127**.22
self-esteem programmes **117**.13, 15
and self-harm **136**.7
sexual exploitation of **99**.16, 20, 21-2
sexualisation of **154**.10
and smoking **145**.2, 5
and sport **118**.20
street children **99**.18-19
violence against **154**.13-14; **155**.26
glandular fever **123**.5
glass **161**.5, 22
recycling **161**.24, 27
glass ceiling **107**.9; **154**.38
for homosexuals **153**.39
glass cliff **107**.9; **154**.34
global citizenship **131**.37
Global Gag Rule **126**.19
global gender inequality **154**.12-14
global inequality **160**.26, 29
global interdependence **146**.4-6

Volume numbers appear first (in bold) followed by page numbers; a change in volume number is preceded by a semi-colon.

Vol. **74** Money Matters
Vol. **76** The Water Crisis
Vol. **78** Threatened Species
Vol. **81** Alternative Therapies
Vol. **82** Protecting our Privacy
Vol. **85** The Housing Crisis
Vol. **88** Food and Nutrition
Vol. **89** Refugees
Vol. **96** Preventing Sexual Diseases
Vol. **97** Energy Matters
Vol. **99** Exploited Children
Vol. **100** Stress and Anxiety
Vol. **103** Animal Rights
Vol. **106** Trends in Marriage
Vol. **107** Work Issues
Vol. **115** Racial Discrimination
Vol. **116** Grief and Loss
Vol. **117** Self-Esteem and Body Image
Vol. **118** Focus on Sport
Vol. **119** Transport Trends
Vol. **120** The Human Rights Issue
Vol. **121** The Censorship Debate

Vol. **122** Bullying
Vol. **123** Young People and Health
Vol. **124** Parenting Issues
Vol. **125** Understanding Depression
Vol. **126** The Abortion Debate
Vol. **127** Eating Disorders
Vol. **128** The Cannabis Issue
Vol. **129** Gambling Trends
Vol. **130** Homelessness
Vol. **131** Citizenship and National Identity
Vol. **132** Child Abuse
Vol. **133** Teen Pregnancy and Lone Parents
Vol. **134** Customers and Consumerism
Vol. **135** Coping with Disability
Vol. **136** Self-Harm
Vol. **137** Crime and Anti-Social Behaviour
Vol. **138** A Genetically Modified Future?
Vol. **139** The Education Problem
Vol. **140** Vegetarian and Vegan Diets
Vol. **141** Mental Health
Vol. **142** Media Issues
Vol. **143** Problem Drinking

Vol. **144** The Cloning Debate
Vol. **145** Smoking Trends
Vol. **146** Sustainability and Environment
Vol. **147** The Terrorism Problem
Vol. **148** Religious Beliefs
Vol. **149** A Classless Society?
Vol. **150** Migration and Population
Vol. **151** Climate Change
Vol. **152** Euthanasia and the Right to Die
Vol. **153** Sexual Orientation and Society
Vol. **154** The Gender Gap
Vol. **155** Domestic Abuse
Vol. **156** Travel and Tourism
Vol. **157** The Problem of Globalisation
Vol. **158** The Internet Revolution
Vol. **159** An Ageing Population
Vol. **160** Poverty and Exclusion
Vol. **161** Waste Issues
Vol. **162** Staying Fit
Vol. **163** Drugs in the UK

global positioning satellites and road charging **119**.36
global poverty **160**.25-39
global trade, attitudes to **157**.39
global warming **151**.1
    and air travel **156**.26
    and biodiversity **146**.19
    causes of **151**.3-4, 5-6
    computer models **151**.5
    and consumer behaviour **134**.31
    costs **151**.8
    denial of **151**.14-15
    effects of **151**.1, 7, 8
    and energy efficiency **97**.29
    evidence for **151**.1, 3
    and renewable energy **97**.8
globalisation **157**.1-15
    benefits **157**.1, 25, 26-7
    and child labour **99**.14
    concerns about **157**.3, 9-11, 25, 37-8
    definition **157**.1, 2, 3, 6, 12
    and developing countries **157**.25
    and economic growth **157**.1
    effects of **157**.1, 3-4, 9-11, 12, 37-8
    and the environment **157**.10
    facts **157**.2
    and inequality **157**.3-4, 9
    monoculture fears **157**.11
    and multinationals **157**.30-31
    and trade **157**.17-39
    types **157**.2
'glorifying terrorism' offence **121**.9
glucose **88**.15
GM crops *see* genetically modified (GM) crops
GMOs *see* genetically modified organisms
GNP (Gross National Product) **157**.6
GNVQs (General National Vocational Qualifications) **139**.4
Golden Rule **148**.8-9, 15-16
gonorrhoea **96**.2, 3, 4, 8, 9, 10
    and HIV **96**.12
governance benefits of globalisation **157**.1
Government
    abortion time-limit review **126**.36-7
    control of the media **121**.1; **142**.2
    finance, and smoking **145**.1
    media censorship **121**.37
    media influence **142**.2
    Parliament **131**.15
    spending on aid **157**.10
    use of the media **121**.17-18
Government policies
    crime, public confidence in **137**.5
    on drugs **163**.22-4
    on families
        children and divorce **106**.35-6
        and cohabitees **106**.7-8
        and marriage **106**.31
        and relationship support **106**.29-30
    on genetically modified crops **138**.5
    on health **162**.4-5, 9-10, 17-18, 22-3
    on homelessness **130**.16, 28, 33
    housing

        and the environment **85**.15
        in rural areas **85**.5, 27-8, 31
        social housing **130**.16, 33
    on ID cards **82**.7-12
    on plastic bags **161**.14
    to reduce educational attainment gap **149**.30, 37-8
    sensible drinking guidelines *see* daily benchmarks on alcohol consumption
    on surveillance **82**.1-3, 22, 23
    waste strategy **161**.20
    on young people's health **123**.31
governments
    role in globalisation **157**.4
    and the World Trade Organisation **157**.21
GPs (general practitioners)
    and bereavement support **116**.2
    and complementary medicine **81**.21, 29, 34
    and disability support **135**.4
    and eating disorders **127**.28
    reporting a death **116**.31
    seeking help for stress from **100**.2, 33, 34
graduates **107**.14-15, 35-6
    basic skills concerns **139**.17
    debt **139**.35
    earnings **139**.35, 36, 37
    employment **139**.33
        and social class **149**.2
    incentives for teacher training **139**.12
    starting salaries **74**.31; **139**.35, 36
grandparents
    and childcare **124**.1, 37-8
    opinions of parenting skills **124**.2
grants, student **139**.34
graves **116**.37
    visiting **116**.16
Green Belt land **85**.28, 30, 31, 39
green burials **116**.39
green cars *see* fuel efficient cars
green consumerism **146**.38-9
green exercise and mental well-being **117**.38
green space and mental health **141**.35
green waste **161**.28-9, 30
greenfield sites
    house-building on **85**.9, 25
    guidelines on **85**.28
    and housing density **85**.34
    and urban renewal **85**.35
greenhouse effect **151**.1, 3
greenhouse gases **151**.1, 7
    emission reduction targets **146**.8-9
    emissions, China **146**.5
    emissions from tourism **156**.25
    sequestration **151**.26
greenwashing **156**.24
grief **116**.1-2, 3-5, 7-9
    counselling **116**.6
    importance of grieving **116**.3
    length of grieving process **116**.4-5
    public **116**.17-18
    and traumatic bereavement **116**.10-11
    and young people **116**.19-28

grooming, online **132**.33
Gross Domestic Product (GDP) **157**.6
Gross National Product (GNP) **157**.6
growth and nutrition, teenagers **123**.6-7
guarantees, consumer rights **134**.18-19
guilt, feelings after bereavement **116**.4, 11, 19
    children **116**.27
    and traumatic bereavement **116**.11
GURTs (Genetic Use Restriction Technologies) **138**.18
gym drugs **118**.35
Gypsy/Roma children and education **115**.18

H

habitat loss
    and endangered wildlife in Britain **78**.30-1, 32
haematopoietic cell transplantation (HTD) **144**.21
hair, stem cell therapy **144**.22
hallucinogens (psychedelics) **163**.2, 6
hangovers and exercise **162**.32
happiness, increasing **117**.6
happy slapping **122**.5, 26
haram foods, Islam **148**.11
harassment **122**.30
    racial **115**.8
    on grounds of sexual orientation **153**.38
hard segregation **115**.28
hare coursing **103**.25, 26, 27
hashish (cannabis resins) **128**.1, 3, 6, 23
hazardous waste **161**.6, 32
hazardous work
    and child labour **99**.1, 2, 3
    domestic labour **99**.7
head injuries and risk of Alzheimer's disease **159**.36
health
    and alcohol **143**.4, 6, 7, 9-10, 27
    and cannabis **163**.6, 9, 35
        and the immune system **128**.19
        and lung cancer **128**.17, 19, 28
        respiratory effects **128**.18-19
        reclassification of **128**.30-32, 38

census information **150**.36
and children's rights **120**.11
and cloning **144**.2, 6, 39
and compulsive exercise **162**.39
and cycling **119**.39
and drugs
    amphetamines **163**.4-5
    cocaine **163**.4
    ecstasy **163**.5, 10
    LSD **163**.6
    opiates **163**.5
    solvents **163**.6
and eating disorders **127**.4-5
gender gap **154**.6
and GM crops **138**.9-10
government strategies **162**.4-5, 9-10, 17-18, 22-3
holidays **156**.4-5
and homeless people **130**.20
    children **130**.23
    older people **130**.17
and meat consumption **140**.12, 13, 21
and migrants **150**.21-3
and obesity **123**.31; **127**.32, 34; **162**.1-2, 5, 6, 7, 19, 25
older people **159**.4, 6, 8, 34
and physical activity **118**.3, 20
and poverty **160**.2
and self-esteem **117**.31, 33
and smoking **145**.25-39
    benefits of giving up **145**.27, 35
    children **145**.2
    developing countries **145**.23
    passive smoking **145**.2, 28-9
    and smoking ban **145**.12
and social class **149**.13-14
students **123**.4-5
and traffic increase **119**.1
and traffic pollution **119**.13-14, 31
and vegetarian diets **140**.1, 2-3, 5, 11
and walking to school **119**.27, 31
worries, young people **123**.3
young carers **141**.24
health beliefs **150**.21-2

Volume numbers appear first (in bold) followed by page numbers; a change in volume number is preceded by a semi-colon.

Vol. **74** Money Matters
Vol. **76** The Water Crisis
Vol. **78** Threatened Species
Vol. **81** Alternative Therapies
Vol. **82** Protecting our Privacy
Vol. **85** The Housing Crisis
Vol. **88** Food and Nutrition
Vol. **89** Refugees
Vol. **96** Preventing Sexual Diseases
Vol. **97** Energy Matters
Vol. **99** Exploited Children
Vol. **100** Stress and Anxiety
Vol. **103** Animal Rights
Vol. **106** Trends in Marriage
Vol. **107** Work Issues
Vol. **115** Racial Discrimination
Vol. **116** Grief and Loss
Vol. **117** Self-Esteem and Body Image
Vol. **118** Focus on Sport
Vol. **119** Transport Trends
Vol. **120** The Human Rights Issue
Vol. **121** The Censorship Debate

Vol. **122** Bullying
Vol. **123** Young People and Health
Vol. **124** Parenting Issues
Vol. **125** Understanding Depression
Vol. **126** The Abortion Debate
Vol. **127** Eating Disorders
Vol. **128** The Cannabis Issue
Vol. **129** Gambling Trends
Vol. **130** Homelessness
Vol. **131** Citizenship and National Identity
Vol. **132** Child Abuse
Vol. **133** Teen Pregnancy and Lone Parents
Vol. **134** Customers and Consumerism
Vol. **135** Coping with Disability
Vol. **136** Self-Harm
Vol. **137** Crime and Anti-Social Behaviour
Vol. **138** A Genetically Modified Future?
Vol. **139** The Education Problem
Vol. **140** Vegetarian and Vegan Diets
Vol. **141** Mental Health
Vol. **142** Media Issues
Vol. **143** Problem Drinking

Vol. **144** The Cloning Debate
Vol. **145** Smoking Trends
Vol. **146** Sustainability and Environment
Vol. **147** The Terrorism Problem
Vol. **148** Religious Beliefs
Vol. **149** A Classless Society?
Vol. **150** Migration and Population
Vol. **151** Climate Change
Vol. **152** Euthanasia and the Right to Die
Vol. **153** Sexual Orientation and Society
Vol. **154** The Gender Gap
Vol. **155** Domestic Abuse
Vol. **156** Travel and Tourism
Vol. **157** The Problem of Globalisation
Vol. **158** The Internet Revolution
Vol. **159** An Ageing Population
Vol. **160** Poverty and Exclusion
Vol. **161** Waste Issues
Vol. **162** Staying Fit
Vol. **163** Drugs in the UK

health care
    costs, obesity **127**.33-4, 37
    and disabled people **135**.4; 20
    effect of legalising euthanasia **152**.4
    information and the media **117**.18
    older people **159**.6
    and refugees **89**.19-20
    UK dependence on workers from overseas **146**.6
health cure scams **134**.27
health education on smoking **145**.3, 5
health and safety issues, WTO **157**.23
health warnings on alcohol **143**.30, 31, 32
health and wellness holidays **156**.4-5
healthy eating **88**.1-2, 5-7; **127**.23
    children **162**.25-6
    as help for depression **125**.3, 39
    government strategies **162**.10, 17-18
    and meat consumption **140**.12, 14, 21
    and social class **162**.13-14
    and stress relief **100**.30, 31, 34, 35, 38-9
    tyranny **162**.16
    and vegetarian diets **140**.1, 3-4, , 6, 7, 10, 11
    young people **123**.1
healthy weight maintenance *see* weight management
hearing, stem cell therapy **144**.22
heart attacks and cycling **119**.39
heart disease
    and depression **125**.5
    and eating disorders **127**.5
    and medical research **103**.12, 18
    and obesity **162**.7
    protective effect of alcohol **143**.7, 27
    stem cell therapy **144**.22, 23, 28
    and stress **100**.19
heatstroke and ecstasy **163**.10
heavy metals, air pollution **146**.36
hemp **128**.6, 34
hens
    genetically modified **138**.20-21
    welfare **140**.38-9
hepatitis **103**.13
    and HIV **96**.10, 13
herbal cannabis (marijuana/grass) **128**.2, 3, 6, 23
    seizures of **128**.31
herbal medicine **81**.4, 11, 23, 36
    banned herbs **81**.24
    Chinese **81**.14-15
    defining **81**.2, 11
    effectiveness of **81**.24
    expenditure on **81**.37
    and multiple sclerosis **81**.30
    and pharmaceutical drugs **81**.11
    regulation of **81**.23
    and scientists **81**.28, 29
herbicide tolerance **138**.4
heredity
    and Alzheimer's disease **159**.36
    and mental illness **141**.24
heroin **163**.5
    and cannabis use **128**.9-10
    market trends **163**.25

herpes *see* genital herpes
hidden homelessness **130**.3, 13, 21-2
high blood pressure (hypertension) **88**.2, 9, 16
    and depression **125**.5
High Court **137**.36
higher education **139**.2, 29-39
    degree results **139**.33
    funding **139**.34
    and social class **149**.1-2
    statistics **139**.32
Highers (exams) **139**.4
Hinduism **148**.2-3
    and abortion and contraception **126**.2-3
    and faith schools **148**.35-6
    festivals **148**.3
    food rules **148**.3, 11
    funerals **116**.34; **148**.3
hire purchase **134**.22
history, British, importance of teaching **131**.7
HIV (Human Immunodeficiency Virus) **96**.7, 14-39
    and anti-gay prejudice **153**.2
    and babies **96**.31, 39
    and bacterial STIs **96**.12
    and child labour **99**.3
    and child soldiers **99**.31
    and children **96**.20, 39
    clinics **96**.10
    defining **96**.14
    Government policies on **96**.16, 39
    and 'health tourism' **96**.21, 39
    and hepatitis **96**.10, 13
    increase in diagnoses **96**.8, 23, 39
    and migrant population **150**.22-3
    Millennium Development Goals **160**.32
    older people as carers **159**.5
    and parents of lesbians and gay people **153**.9
    prevention **96**.32-4
        and condoms **96**.12, 14, 16, 24, 25, 29, 30, 32, 33, 34
        future of **96**.34
        and treatment **96**.32, 37, 38-9
    and the sexual exploitation of children **99**.16, 24
    signs and symptoms **96**.7
    testing for **96**.1, 7, 8, 14, 16
    transmission **96**.14, 18
    treatments **96**.7, 14-15, 20-1
        antiretroviral therapy (ART) **96**.36, 37, 38, 39
        closing the treatment gap **96**.36-7
        combination therapy **96**.15
        costs of **96**.21
        drugs from GM (pharmed) crops **138**.21, 22
        and prevention **96**.32, 37, 38-9
        vaccines **96**.33-4
    UK statistics **96**.20-2, 23
    and unprotected sex **96**.12, 16, 28
    and women **96**.17, 20, 24-5, 29, 30-1
        pregnant **96**.16, 22, 23, 31, 38
    and young people **96**.17, 24-9, 38
        and alcohol and drug use **96**.26
        education **96**.26
        young women **96**.24-5, 27-8, 29
    see also AIDS

holidays

    and bullying **122**.12

    and climate change concerns **156**.28-30

    destinations **156**.3

    ethical **134**.30

    expenditure on **134**.3

    as status symbols **156**.5

Holocaust denial **121**.8, 12-13

home abortions **126**.32-4

home care services **159**.4

    costs **159**.26

home expenditure, ethical **134**.32

home furnishings, spending on **134**.4

home insulation **151**.38, 39

home learning **139**.27-8

Home Office and counter-terrorism **147**.2

home ownership and social class **149**.20

    attitudes to moving home **149**.26

home schooling **139**.27

home and sex education **133**.15

homeless households **85**.11; **130**.1

homeless young people **130**.14-15, 21-7

    and debt **130**.24-6

    hidden homelessness **130**.21-2

    homelessness causes **130**.21

    mental health **130**.27

homelessness

    and affordable housing **130**.8, 16, 23, 33

    and beggars **130**.12

    causes **130**.3, 6, 10-11

        young people **130**.21

    and children **130**.23

    defining **130**.1-3

    and drug use **130**.11, 20

    and employment **130**.15, 36-7

    and health **130**.20

        children **130**.23

        older people **130**.17

    government strategies **130**.16, 28, 33

    help for homeless people **130**.21-2, 28-39

    hidden homeless **130**.3, 13, 21-2

    history of **130**.4

intentionally homeless **130**.2

legislation

    England and Wales **130**.28

    Scotland **130**.5

and local authorities **130**.2-3, 28, 29-30

and mental health problems **130**.20

    street homeless **130**.11

    young people **130**.27

myths and facts **130**.7

and older people **130**.17-18; **159**.4

preventing **130**.28-30

priority needs homeless **130**.2

reduction in **130**.16

repeat homelessness **130**.34

risk factors **130**.3

rough sleeping **130**.6, 9-12

Scotland **130**.5-6

statistics **130**.13-15, 22

homeopathy **81**.12-13, 23, 36

    and cancer **81**.32

    defining **81**.2, 12

    effectiveness of **81**.22, 24, 28

    expenditure on **81**.37

    and the placebo effect **81**.26

    and scientists **81**.28-9

    treatments **81**.12-13

homestays **156**.24

homework **139**.27, 28

homeworking **107**.12, 14-15, 19-20, 22

    scams **134**.27

homophobia **153**.13

    in football **118**.17

    homophobic bullying **122**.3; **153**.14-18

    and violence **137**.8

homosexuality **153**.1-3

    causes **153**.3, 6, 7

    coming out **153**.3, 8

    'correction' of **153**.3

    discrimination **153**.2-3, 27-8

    genetic factors **153**.6, 7

    and the media **142**.39; **153**.23-5

    and mental disorder **153**.3, 4

Volume numbers appear first (in bold) followed by page numbers; a change in volume number is preceded by a semi-colon.

Vol. **74** Money Matters

Vol. **76** The Water Crisis

Vol. **78** Threatened Species

Vol. **81** Alternative Therapies

Vol. **82** Protecting our Privacy

Vol. **85** The Housing Crisis

Vol. **88** Food and Nutrition

Vol. **89** Refugees

Vol. **96** Preventing Sexual Diseases

Vol. **97** Energy Matters

Vol. **99** Exploited Children

Vol. **100** Stress and Anxiety

Vol. **103** Animal Rights

Vol. **106** Trends in Marriage

Vol. **107** Work Issues

Vol. **115** Racial Discrimination

Vol. **116** Grief and Loss

Vol. **117** Self-Esteem and Body Image

Vol. **118** Focus on Sport

Vol. **119** Transport Trends

Vol. **120** The Human Rights Issue

Vol. **121** The Censorship Debate

Vol. **122** Bullying

Vol. **123** Young People and Health

Vol. **124** Parenting Issues

Vol. **125** Understanding Depression

Vol. **126** The Abortion Debate

Vol. **127** Eating Disorders

Vol. **128** The Cannabis Issue

Vol. **129** Gambling Trends

Vol. **130** Homelessness

Vol. **131** Citizenship and National Identity

Vol. **132** Child Abuse

Vol. **133** Teen Pregnancy and Lone Parents

Vol. **134** Customers and Consumerism

Vol. **135** Coping with Disability

Vol. **136** Self-Harm

Vol. **137** Crime and Anti-Social Behaviour

Vol. **138** A Genetically Modified Future?

Vol. **139** The Education Problem

Vol. **140** Vegetarian and Vegan Diets

Vol. **141** Mental Health

Vol. **142** Media Issues

Vol. **143** Problem Drinking

Vol. **144** The Cloning Debate

Vol. **145** Smoking Trends

Vol. **146** Sustainability and Environment

Vol. **147** The Terrorism Problem

Vol. **148** Religious Beliefs

Vol. **149** A Classless Society?

Vol. **150** Migration and Population

Vol. **151** Climate Change

Vol. **152** Euthanasia and the Right to Die

Vol. **153** Sexual Orientation and Society

Vol. **154** The Gender Gap

Vol. **155** Domestic Abuse

Vol. **156** Travel and Tourism

Vol. **157** The Problem of Globalisation

Vol. **158** The Internet Revolution

Vol. **159** An Ageing Population

Vol. **160** Poverty and Exclusion

Vol. **161** Waste Issues

Vol. **162** Staying Fit

Vol. **163** Drugs in the UK

and young people **123**.21; **133**.2
hooliganism, football **118**.7, 8
hormonal methods of contraception **123**.23
hormones
    and appetite regulation **127**.38-9
    use in sport **118**.37
horse meat as food **140**.18
hospitals
    admission for manic depression **125**.19-20
    admission for self-harm **136**.4, 10
    death, formal procedures **116**.31
hostels **130**.31
hotels, limiting environmental impact **156**.24
hours of work **107**.2, 3, 6, 14, 24
    fathers **124**.11
    full-time mothers **124**.12
House of Commons **131**.15
House of Lords **131**.15
house prices **85**.1, 3-4; **134**.25
    and first-time buyers **85**.6, 7
    and homelessness **130**.8
    regional differences in **85**.3-4, 6, 8
    and single people **85**.7
household crime **137**.4
    racial identity of victims **115**.10
household tasks and working parents **124**.11
household waste **161**.1, 5, 6, 18-19, 31
    composition of **161**.1
households
    and energy efficiency **97**.2, 27-30, 31, 32-3; **151**.39
    gender roles **154**.15, 21
    growth in numbers of **85**.1-2, 3, 29
      and the need for new homes **85**.8-9, 20
    income inequalities **160**.6-7
    minimum standard income **160**.8
    size of **106**.2, 3
    structure and poverty **160**.2
housework
    and gender **154**.15
    parents, time spent on **124**.11
housing
    advice centres **130**.29
    age of houses in the UK **85**.30
    census information **150**.36
    debt **134**.23
    and the environment **85**.14-15, 26
    expenditure **134**.4
    home ownership in the UK **85**.30
      and social class **149**.20, 26
    housing crisis 'backlog' **85**.2
    investment in as a share of gross domestic product **85**.3
    in London **85**.10-13, 16-17
    and lone parents **133**.37
    need for new homes **85**.1-3, 8-9
      numbers required **85**.9, 20
      and planning laws **85**.20
      targets **85**.1
    and 'neighbourhood collapse' **85**.38
    new house-building
      in cities **85**.25
      and housing density **85**.25, 34

    in the M11 region **85**.18, 22, 26, 27, 33
    numbers being built **85**.3
    and planning permission **85**.35
    in the Thames Gateway **85**.21-4, 26, 33
    older people **159**.4
    rented accommodation shortage **130**.8
    shortage **130**.8, 16, 30
    size of houses in the UK **85**.30
    social housing
      shortage **130**.8, 23
      Government strategy **130**.16, 33
housing associations
    and house-building **85**.24
    in London
      and shared ownership houses **85**.11
      and unfit dwellings **85**.12
    and private developers **85**.19
Housing Benefit **133**.34-5; **135**.5
    problems, and homelessness **130**.9
human-animal embryos **144**.9, 11, 13, 14, 20
human-ape hybrids **144**.11
human cloning **144**.1-14
    ethical issues **144**.2-3, 5-6, 7-8
    public attitudes **144**.35
human dignity
    and cloning **144**.3
    and inter-species mixing **144**.12
human embryos
    stem cells *see* embryonic stem cells
    hybrid embryos **144**.9, 11, 13, 14, 20
human genes
    in bacteria **144**.11
    in mice **144**.11
human growth hormones (HGHs) and sport **118**.37
human reproductive cloning
    autonomy issues **144**.3
    benefits **144**.2
    and dignity **144**.3
    ethical concerns **144**.2-3, 8
human rights **120**.23-7
    and animal rights **103**.33
    and cartoons of Mohammed **121**.11-12
    and CCTV **82**.24
    and child labour **99**.4, 6
      domestic work **99**.8
    and child soldiers **99**.30, 31-2
    and children's rights **120**.1-22
    and corporal punishment **132**.9, 12-13, 16-17
    female migrants **150**.15
    and identity cards **120**.37
    and privacy **82**.4-5, 18
    and refugees **120**.31
    smoking ban challenge **145**.15
    and surveillance **120**.33
    water as a human right **76**.24-5, 32
    and workers **120**.28-31
Human Rights, Universal Declaration of **120**.23-5
Human Rights Act **82**.18, 24, 39; **120**.25-7
    and workplace monitoring **82**.29; **120**.33
human values **148**.15
humanism

and abortion **126**.4-5
and animal welfare **140**.31-3
and embryo research **144**.7-8
and ethics **148**.13-16
funerals **116**.35
and the Golden Rule **148**.8, 15-16
motivation **148**.14
humidity, global increase **151**.2
hunger **160**.28
Millennium Development Goals **160**.30
hunting **103**.24-31
arguments against **103**.26
arguments for **103**.24-5
badger digging **103**.28
before the ban **103**.26
for bushmeat **78**.18
clothes worn **103**.25
and the control of wild animals **103**.25
and cruelty **103**.25, 26
deer hunting **103**.24, 28
with helicopters **103**.29
draghunting **103**.24-5, 26
as food source **140**.17
fox numbers and the ban on **103**.26
hare coursing **103**.25, 26, 27
history of the abolition of **103**.27-8
and hounds **103**.24
hunt saboteurs **103**.28, 30
killing the fox **103**.24
law on (Hunting Act 2004) **103**.26, 27
testing enforcement of **103**.31
and mammals in the UK **78**.32
otter hunting **103**.28
public attitudes to **103**.24, 25
questions and answers on **103**.24-5
whales **78**.6, 13, 14
of wildlife **78**.2, 4-5, 5-6
hybrid animals **144**.10-12
hybrid embryos **144**.9, 11, 13, 14, 20
hybrid vehicles **119**.22
hybridisation **138**.12-13
hydrocarbon (HC) emissions **119**.15

hypertension *see* high blood pressure

I

identity
British identity of non-white ethnic groups **115**.38
identity confusion **149**.4-5
protection in interviews **142**.12
protection online **158**.10
racial, victims of crime **115**.10
religious **115**.5, 26
and social class **149**.3, 4, 18, 19, 24
identity (ID) cards **82**.1, 2, 7-12; **120**.34, 35-6; **131**.13-14
and biometric data **82**.9, 10, 12
and bogus asylum seekers **82**.7, 8
and civil liberties **82**.11-12
and electronic fraud **82**.11
fee to be charged for **82**.7, 8, 10
fraud **82**.7, 8
and health and welfare benefit abuse **82**.7, 8, 9
and human rights **120**.37
and identity fraud **82**.11, 12
opposition to **82**.7, 8
and personal freedom **82**.8
public attitudes to **82**.7-8
identity disorders **141**.11
identity theft **134**.27-8, 28-9; **158**.3, 32, 33-4
illegal broadcasting **142**.7
illegal dumping *see* fly-tipping
illegal employment **89**.10-11, 30-1
illegal immigrants **89**.11, 30-1
attitudes to **150**.3
illegal parking **119**.9
illegal planting of GM crops **138**.19
illegal wildlife trade souvenirs **156**.32
illness
and depression **125**.2, 5-6
as reason for not exercising **162**.31
images, effects on young people's behaviour **145**.6
IMF (International Monetary Fund) **157**.6, 10, 17
immigration

Volume numbers appear first (in bold) followed by page numbers; a change in volume number is preceded by a semi-colon.

Vol. **74** Money Matters
Vol. **76** The Water Crisis
Vol. **78** Threatened Species
Vol. **81** Alternative Therapies
Vol. **82** Protecting our Privacy
Vol. **85** The Housing Crisis
Vol. **88** Food and Nutrition
Vol. **89** Refugees
Vol. **96** Preventing Sexual Diseases
Vol. **97** Energy Matters
Vol. **99** Exploited Children
Vol. **100** Stress and Anxiety
Vol. **103** Animal Rights
Vol. **106** Trends in Marriage
Vol. **107** Work Issues
Vol. **115** Racial Discrimination
Vol. **116** Grief and Loss
Vol. **117** Self-Esteem and Body Image
Vol. **118** Focus on Sport
Vol. **119** Transport Trends
Vol. **120** The Human Rights Issue
Vol. **121** The Censorship Debate

Vol. **122** Bullying
Vol. **123** Young People and Health
Vol. **124** Parenting Issues
Vol. **125** Understanding Depression
Vol. **126** The Abortion Debate
Vol. **127** Eating Disorders
Vol. **128** The Cannabis Issue
Vol. **129** Gambling Trends
Vol. **130** Homelessness
Vol. **131** Citizenship and National Identity
Vol. **132** Child Abuse
Vol. **133** Teen Pregnancy and Lone Parents
Vol. **134** Customers and Consumerism
Vol. **135** Coping with Disability
Vol. **136** Self-Harm
Vol. **137** Crime and Anti-Social Behaviour
Vol. **138** A Genetically Modified Future?
Vol. **139** The Education Problem
Vol. **140** Vegetarian and Vegan Diets
Vol. **141** Mental Health
Vol. **142** Media Issues
Vol. **143** Problem Drinking

Vol. **144** The Cloning Debate
Vol. **145** Smoking Trends
Vol. **146** Sustainability and Environment
Vol. **147** The Terrorism Problem
Vol. **148** Religious Beliefs
Vol. **149** A Classless Society?
Vol. **150** Migration and Population
Vol. **151** Climate Change
Vol. **152** Euthanasia and the Right to Die
Vol. **153** Sexual Orientation and Society
Vol. **154** The Gender Gap
Vol. **155** Domestic Abuse
Vol. **156** Travel and Tourism
Vol. **157** The Problem of Globalisation
Vol. **158** The Internet Revolution
Vol. **159** An Ageing Population
Vol. **160** Poverty and Exclusion
Vol. **161** Waste Issues
Vol. **162** Staying Fit
Vol. **163** Drugs in the UK

attitudes to **150**.3, 13-14, 17, 18-19

church attendance of immigrants **148**.23-4

definition **150**.21

illegal immigrants **89**.11, 30-1

lack of accurate data **150**.19

and globalisation **157**.37

and population growth, UK **150**.16

problems of **150**.16-17

quota system proposal **131**.10

statistics, UK **150**.4, 8-9

worldwide **150**.33

immune system, effect of cannabis **128**.19

immunization and animal diseases **103**.12

imports

UK dependence on **146**.4-6

imprisonment *see* prison

in vitro (in glass) research **103**.14, 18, 19

inactivity

children **162**.13, 15, 25

health effects **162**.11

Incapacity Benefit **135**.5

incentives

for reducing waste **161**.38

for weight loss **162**.22-3

incest **132**.26

incineration of waste **161**.7

incitement to religious hatred **148**.29

inclusion

and sport **118**.12

disabled people **118**.22

ethnic minorities **118**.13-16

women **118**.18-22

inclusive education **135**.37-9

and behavioural problems **120**.16

Income Support **133**.33; **135**.5

incomes **107**.2, 13

and children's educational attainment **149**.25

global **157**.2

inequalities **160**.6, 7

lone-parent families **124**.35; **133**.28, 30

minimum standard **160**.8

minimum wage **107**.31

and part-time working **107**.17

pensioners **159**.3

and social class **149**.19, 20

stress and income levels **100**.13

and voter turnout **131**.19

independence, encouraging children's **124**.13-14

independent living and learning disabilities **135**.34-5

independent schools and SEN provision **135**.36

index of isolation **115**.32

index of segregation **115**.31-2

indigenous people and poverty **160**.25

indirect discrimination

racial **115**.7, 11

on sexuality **153**.38

indoor (contained) GMOs **138**.12

industry

and child labour **99**.1, 2

motivations for GM development **138**.8

water consumption **76**.2, 8, 36

water pollution **76**.11

inequality

attitudes to **160**.9

in climate change effects **151**.11, 19

effect of free trade **157**.13, 23-4

gender *see* gender gap

global **160**.26, 28

and globalisation **157**.2, 3-4, 9

of incomes **160**.6, 7

and segregation **115**.30, 31, 32

and tourism **156**.20

infection risk of abortion **126**.14

infections

as cause of anorexia **127**.12

as cause of depression **125**.5

infertility

and anti-abortion movement **126**.25

information

children's rights to **120**.10

as consumer right **134**.1-2

for disabled children **135**.21

and ethical consumerism **134**.33-4

personal, control of **158**.31-4

and the web **158**.2

information technology (IT)

benefits **157**.1

educational projects **82**.28

and globalisation **157**.1, 2, 15

inherited learning disability **135**.33

injectable hormonal contraceptive **123**.23

injury as reason for not exercising **162**.32

injuries from domestic violence **155**.30

inner city areas, voter turnout **131**.19

inquests **116**.32

insects, GM viral infections **138**.13-14

insecurity

and bullying **122**.8

feelings after bereavement **116**.4

insomnia

and stress **100**.19, 29

instant justice by police, proposal **137**.34

instant messaging (IM) and bullying **122**.20, 21

institutional disablism **135**.28

institutional prejudice in childhood, and low self-esteem **117**.32

institutions, leaving, as cause of homelessness **130**. 11

instructions to discriminate **115**.12

insulation, home **151**.38, 39

insulin, effect of nicotine **145**.26

insurance

car insurance offences **119**.9

and homeworking **107**.20

life insurance **106**.14

and money management **106**.14

and privacy rights **82**.25-6

and young people **74**.2, 15

integrated medicine/healthcare **81**.36-8

integration, racial *see* racial integration

intellectual property rights *see* patents

intelligent design **148**.37-9

intelligent speed adaptation technology **119**.18

intelligent transport systems **119**.38

intentionally homeless people **130**. 2
interactive gambling **129**.17-26
interdependence, global **146**.4-6
interest free credit **134**.22
interest rates
    credit cards **74**.26, 27
    and mortgage repayments **85**.6
    and savings **74**.24
interests, and improving self-esteem **117**.6, 8, 33
inter-ethnic marriages **115**.25
interfaith relations, young people **148**.32-3
intergender **153**.13
Intermix, website for mixed-race families **124**.36-7
internally displaced persons **89**.1, 6, 8-9
international anti-doping policy **118**.27-8, 31-2
international companies *see* multinational corporations
international law and child labour **120**.20
International Monetary Fund (IMF) *see* IMF
International Olympic Committee (IOC), anti-doping
    initiatives **118**.25
international students **139**.30, 31, 32
    and terrorism **147**.13-14
international terrorism, history of **147**.4-5
international trade **157**.17-39
    ecologically wasteful **146**.5
    facts **157**.19
    and genetic modification **138**.27
    and poverty **157**.26-7; **160**.37-8
    and taxes **157**.12-13
    UK dependence on **146**.4-6
Internet
    addiction **142**.37; **158**.38-9
    advertising **158**.5
    anti-extremism projects **147**.34
    banking **74**.2
    broadband access **158**.5-6, 17, 18
    bullying by e-mail **122**.5, 19, 21
    and censorship **121**.18-21
        China **121**.2, 19-20; **158**.37
    and child sex abuse **132**.30, 31-2, 33
    and children and young people **158**.20-21
    development of **158**.1

and divorce rates **106**.31
downloading **158**.33, 35-6
and entertainment **158**.21-2
family usage **158**.7-8
filesharing **158**.36
fraud **134**.26-9
future of **158**.25-6
gambling *see* online gambling
and globalisation **157**.1, 2, 15
journalism register **142**.16
and media regulation **142**.2
National Lottery games, and under 16s **129**.12-13
as news source **142**.33
and newspapers **142**.9
and older people **158**.4
online activity **158**.4, 15
    children **158**.20-21
    older people **158**.4
    young people **158**.27
online bullying **122**.19-26
phishing **134**.27-8, 28-9; **158**.33-4
reaching capacity **158**.24
regulation **142**.2
risks **158**.27-39
sex offenders, helpline for **132**.36
and the sexual exploitation of children **99**.16, 21, 24
shopping **158**.3, 30-31
    Europe **134**.15-16
    and gender **134**.16
social networking sites **142**.35, 36, 38; **157**.15
suicide websites **136**.37, 38, 39
surveillance
    and the Government **82**.1, 22, 23
    in the workplace **82**.25, 26, 27, 28; **120**.32
and terrorism **147**.8-9
and travel industry **156**.1, 13, 14
trends **158**.1-26
intersexuality **153**.13
inter-species mixing **144**.10-12
intestinal problems and eating disorders **127**.5
Invalid Care Allowance **135**.5-6
investment scams **134**.27

Volume numbers appear first (in bold) followed by page numbers; a change in volume number is preceded by a semi-colon.

Vol. **74** Money Matters
Vol. **76** The Water Crisis
Vol. **78** Threatened Species
Vol. **81** Alternative Therapies
Vol. **82** Protecting our Privacy
Vol. **85** The Housing Crisis
Vol. **88** Food and Nutrition
Vol. **89** Refugees
Vol. **96** Preventing Sexual Diseases
Vol. **97** Energy Matters
Vol. **99** Exploited Children
Vol. **100** Stress and Anxiety
Vol. **103** Animal Rights
Vol. **106** Trends in Marriage
Vol. **107** Work Issues
Vol. **115** Racial Discrimination
Vol. **116** Grief and Loss
Vol. **117** Self-Esteem and Body Image
Vol. **118** Focus on Sport
Vol. **119** Transport Trends
Vol. **120** The Human Rights Issue
Vol. **121** The Censorship Debate

Vol. **122** Bullying
Vol. **123** Young People and Health
Vol. **124** Parenting Issues
Vol. **125** Understanding Depression
Vol. **126** The Abortion Debate
Vol. **127** Eating Disorders
Vol. **128** The Cannabis Issue
Vol. **129** Gambling Trends
Vol. **130** Homelessness
Vol. **131** Citizenship and National Identity
Vol. **132** Child Abuse
Vol. **133** Teen Pregnancy and Lone Parents
Vol. **134** Customers and Consumerism
Vol. **135** Coping with Disability
Vol. **136** Self-Harm
Vol. **137** Crime and Anti-Social Behaviour
Vol. **138** A Genetically Modified Future?
Vol. **139** The Education Problem
Vol. **140** Vegetarian and Vegan Diets
Vol. **141** Mental Health
Vol. **142** Media Issues
Vol. **143** Problem Drinking

Vol. **144** The Cloning Debate
Vol. **145** Smoking Trends
Vol. **146** Sustainability and Environment
Vol. **147** The Terrorism Problem
Vol. **148** Religious Beliefs
Vol. **149** A Classless Society?
Vol. **150** Migration and Population
Vol. **151** Climate Change
Vol. **152** Euthanasia and the Right to Die
Vol. **153** Sexual Orientation and Society
Vol. **154** The Gender Gap
Vol. **155** Domestic Abuse
Vol. **156** Travel and Tourism
Vol. **157** The Problem of Globalisation
Vol. **158** The Internet Revolution
Vol. **159** An Ageing Population
Vol. **160** Poverty and Exclusion
Vol. **161** Waste Issues
Vol. **162** Staying Fit
Vol. **163** Drugs in the UK

involuntary euthanasia **152**.1
involuntary smoking *see* passive smoking
iodine and vegetarian diet **140**.3
IQ
    and gender **154**.24
    and post traumatic stress disorder **141**.3
    and vegetarian diet **140**.10
iridology **81**.17-18
iris recognition, and identity cards **82**.9, 10, 11, 12
iron in the diet **88**.6, 15
    red meat **140**.12
    sources **140**.4, 7
    teenagers' needs **123**.6
    and vegetarian diet **140**.1, 3, 7
irrigation
    and global water supplies **76**.3, 4, 5, 19
    and water shortages **76**.21
Islam **148**.3-4
    and abortion and contraception **126**.2
    and anti-extremism **147**.34
    and the census **148**.7
    and faith schools **148**.35
    festivals **148**.3
    food rules **148**.3-4; 11
    fundamentalist beliefs of young Muslims **147**.16-17
    funerals **116**.34-5
    mosque governance standards **147**.34
    observance trends, Britain **148**.18-19
    preventing youth extremism **148**.30-31
    public perceptions of **147**.26
    teaching in British Mosques **147**.17-18
    and terrorism **147**.15, 26-7
Islamophobia **115**.36
    and national identity **131**.11
isolation, older people **159**.3, 8, 17, 30

J

Jedism **148**.6-7
jewellery, recycling **161**.24
Jews (Judaism) **148**.4-5
    and abortion and contraception **126**.3
    and the Census (2001) **148**.7
    and faith schools **148**.35
    food rules **148**.4, 10-11
    funerals **116**.33-4
    and racism laws **115**.26
jihad **147**.15
jobs
    distribution inequalities **149**.28
    job hunting **107**.31-2
    job satisfaction **107**.1-2, 13; **154**.18
    job security **107**.1, 2
Jobseekers Allowance **133**.33-4
journal keeping as way of remembrance **116**.16
journalists
    and libel law **142**.27
    protection of sources **142**.22
    regulation **142**.16
    talking to **142**.11-14

journey length trends **119**.29
    travelling to school **119**.30
junk mail **134**.26, 28; **161**.19, 26
justice system
    and children **120**.12
    and gender equality **154**.4

K

ketamine **163**.18-20
Key Stages (schools) **139**.1-2, 5
kidney damage and eating disorders **127**.5
Killing with Kindness campaign **130**.32
killings *see* homicide; murder
kinesiology **81**.2
knee repair, stem cell therapy **144**.21
knife carrying by young people **137**.16
knowledge, globalisation of **157**.1
Kyoto Protocol **151**.2
    Clean Development Mechanism **151**.17
    Kyoto Compliant emission reduction projects **151**.21
    UK target **146**.8

L

labelling
    alcohol **143**.30, 31, 32
    ethical products **134**.34
    GM animal feed **138**.25
    GM food **138**.11, 39
    and low self-esteem **117**.6
    products **134**.1-2
labour migration **150**.1-2
Labour Party, policies on crime **137**.2
lacto-ovo-vegetarians **140**.2
lacto-vegetarians **140**.2
lactose, and vegetarians **140**.19
lads' magazines **142**.29
lager, strength of **143**.1
landfill **146**.23; 1-2, 6-7, 10
    hazardous waste **161**.32
    restoring sites to green space **161**.33
    tax **161**.12, 20, 35
language
    in advertising **134**.9
    barriers to employment **89**.27, 35, 37
    of technology **158**.16-17
    strong language on television **121**.38-9
lanolin, and vegetarians **140**.19
law *see* legislation
law and drugs **163**.1-2, 31-9
law-making process **131**.24
    citizen involvement **131**.25
laxatives, effects **127**.2
lead pollution **146**.36
leadership in sport
    ethnic minorities **118**.13
    women **118**.20
learning

effects of cannabis 128.14
impact on homelessness 130.34-5
learning disabilities 135.33-9
causes 135.33
definition 135.33
management of 135.34-5
and the media 135.35
and education 135.36-9
left-wing terrorism 147.1
legal advice and court hearings 137.26
legal rights, young people 120.7-8
legalising drugs, potential results 163.39
legislation
and abortion 126.5, 6, 7-8, 12
age discrimination 159.10, 11
and alcohol 123.16; 2-3
drink-driving 143.24
young people 143.2, 17
on asylum 89.3-4, 11, 12, 33, 39
blasphemy 121.16
and bullying 122.11
racist bullying 122.4
and cannabis 128.2, 7, 9, 26-38
Civil Partnership Act 153.26-8
on climate change 151.17
Communications Act and media mergers 142.4
and corporal punishment 132.8, 15-17
on crime 137.21, 29-30
and domestic violence 155.2; 28; 37-8
and drugs 163.1-2, 33
on embryo research 144.15, 17, 27-8
Equality Act 153.35
and euthanasia 152.1, 16-18, 29-30
Australia 152.19
Belgium 152.4, 18, 19
Italy 152.10-11
Netherlands 152.4, 18, 19
Scotland 152.17, 29, 30
Switzerland 152.18, 19
US, Oregon state 152.4, 18, 19, 31, 33
and film classification 121.23-5
on food additives 88.39

on food labelling 88.23, 24, 25
and forced marriages 155.17
Freedom of Information Act 142.17-21
on gambling
Gambling Act 129.5, 17, 23
and gambling at work 129.23
online gambling 129.17
on gender discrimination 154.14
on homelessness
England and Wales 130.28
Scotland 130.5
law-making process 131.24
citizen involvement 131.25
libel and journalistic freedom 142.27
libel and slander 142.26
Poor Laws 149.13
Racial and Religious Hatred Bill 121.7, 15
and racism 115.2, 7-8, 26
at work 115.11-12
on religious hatred 115.26; 121.7, 15
Sexual Orientation Regulation 153.35, 36, 37
and sexuality 153.26-39
and smacking 132.8
and smoking
ban on smoking in public places 145.11-17
children 145.3
young people 123.12
and video 121.31
video games classification 121.32
leisure activities
effect of poverty 160.2
older people 159.3, 8
leptin (appetite-suppressing hormone) 127.39
lesbians
definition 153.1
having children 153.20-22, 33-4
and the media 142.39
leukaemia
and medical research 103.12
stem cell therapy 144.21
liability for racism at work 115.12
libel 142.26

Volume numbers appear first (in bold) followed by page numbers; a change in volume number is preceded by a semi-colon.

Vol. 74 Money Matters
Vol. 76 The Water Crisis
Vol. 78 Threatened Species
Vol. 81 Alternative Therapies
Vol. 82 Protecting our Privacy
Vol. 85 The Housing Crisis
Vol. 88 Food and Nutrition
Vol. 89 Refugees
Vol. 96 Preventing Sexual Diseases
Vol. 97 Energy Matters
Vol. 99 Exploited Children
Vol. 100 Stress and Anxiety
Vol. 103 Animal Rights
Vol. 106 Trends in Marriage
Vol. 107 Work Issues
Vol. 115 Racial Discrimination
Vol. 116 Grief and Loss
Vol. 117 Self-Esteem and Body Image
Vol. 118 Focus on Sport
Vol. 119 Transport Trends
Vol. 120 The Human Rights Issue
Vol. 121 The Censorship Debate

Vol. 122 Bullying
Vol. 123 Young People and Health
Vol. 124 Parenting Issues
Vol. 125 Understanding Depression
Vol. 126 The Abortion Debate
Vol. 127 Eating Disorders
Vol. 128 The Cannabis Issue
Vol. 129 Gambling Trends
Vol. 130 Homelessness
Vol. 131 Citizenship and National Identity
Vol. 132 Child Abuse
Vol. 133 Teen Pregnancy and Lone Parents
Vol. 134 Customers and Consumerism
Vol. 135 Coping with Disability
Vol. 136 Self-Harm
Vol. 137 Crime and Anti-Social Behaviour
Vol. 138 A Genetically Modified Future?
Vol. 139 The Education Problem
Vol. 140 Vegetarian and Vegan Diets
Vol. 141 Mental Health
Vol. 142 Media Issues
Vol. 143 Problem Drinking

Vol. 144 The Cloning Debate
Vol. 145 Smoking Trends
Vol. 146 Sustainability and Environment
Vol. 147 The Terrorism Problem
Vol. 148 Religious Beliefs
Vol. 149 A Classless Society?
Vol. 150 Migration and Population
Vol. 151 Climate Change
Vol. 152 Euthanasia and the Right to Die
Vol. 153 Sexual Orientation and Society
Vol. 154 The Gender Gap
Vol. 155 Domestic Abuse
Vol. 156 Travel and Tourism
Vol. 157 The Problem of Globalisation
Vol. 158 The Internet Revolution
Vol. 159 An Ageing Population
Vol. 160 Poverty and Exclusion
Vol. 161 Waste Issues
Vol. 162 Staying Fit
Vol. 163 Drugs in the UK

and journalism **142**.27
Liberal Democrat Party, policies on crime 137.2
liberalisation **157**.12, 20
licence fee, BBC **142**.6
licensing
    alcohol sales **143**.2
    gambling **129**.5, 8, 23
    hybrid embryo research **144**.14
    stem cell research **144**.17, 27-8
licensing hours and crime **143**.23
life chances
    and teenage parenthood **133**.10
life expectancy **150**.32, 35; **159**.6
    and alcohol consumption **143**.13
    and poverty **160**.38
    and smoking **145**.21
    and social class **149**.15
    ways of increasing **159**.32-4
    UK **159**.3, 34
lifestyle
    and ageing **159**.2, 34
    and life expectancy **159**.33-4
    sports **118**.1
    stress and changes in **100**.19
    and weight loss **162**.20
light bulbs, recycling **161**.24
light therapy for Seasonal Affective Disorder **125**.18, 37; **141**.35
listeria **88**.28-9
literacy
    employees' literacy problems **139**.17
    and poverty **160**.28
litter **161**.15-16, 21
liver damage and stem cell therapy **144**.22
living alone
    numbers of people **85**.2
    single men **106**.12
living standards and water consumption **76**.8
living wills *see* advance directives (living wills)
loans
    student **139**.34
local authorities
    duty to house **130**. 2-3
    homelessness prevention funds **130**. 29-30
    homelessness strategies **130**. 28
    and tourism **156**.9
Local Authority care leavers, and homelessness **130**.11, 14
local communities, effects of tourism **156**.22
logging, destructive **146**.30
London
    affordable housing
      and household growth **85**.29
      and poverty **85**.10-12
      supply and demand **85**.13
    bombings
      and faith hate crime **115**.27
      impact on Muslims **115**.36
    congestion charging **119**.12, 38
    counter-terrorism measures **147**.31
    empty houses in **85**.13, 25
    house prices **85**.3, 6
    house-building in

      brownfield versus greenfield debate **85**.16-17
      numbers **85**.11
    and migrant workers **150**.11
    multicultural tolerance **115**.23
    overcrowding and poor housing conditions **85**.11-12
    public opinion on housing **85**.13
lone parents **124**.33-5; **133**.28-38
    benefits available **133**.33-6
    benefits claimed **133**.32, 36
    children of **124**.22, 33-4; **133**.28, 31
    and divorce **124**.33-4
    and employment **133**.28
    help for **133**.37-8
    and household income **133**.28, 30
    and housing advice **133**.37
    statistics **106**.2, 3; **124**.35; **133**.28-32
    teenage **126**.31; **133**.28
loneliness
    feelings after bereavement **116**.4, 19
    older people **159**.3, 8, 17, 30
long-term illness **159**.4
losing weight *see* weight loss
loss on childhood, and low self-esteem **117**.32
lotteries **129**.2
    scams **134**.26
low carbon technologies **97**.4
low impact policing and football hooliganism **118**.8
low income families
    subsidised broadband access **158**.18
low income workers **160**.5
low self-esteem (LSE) **117**.5-8, 31
    and bullying **122**.8
    causes of **117**.31-2
    and eating disorders **127**.2
    and self-harm **136**.2
LPG vehicles **119**.20
LSD **163**.6
lung cancer **145**.34
    and cannabis use **128**.17, 19, 28
luxury holidays **156**.2

M

macrobiotic diet **140**.2
magazines
    influence on body image **117**.11-12, 15
    and sex education **142**.28, 29
magic mushrooms **163**.6
magistrates court **137**.36
magnetic field therapy **81**.30, 31
maintained schools, definition **135**.36
maintenance payments **133**.37
malaria **76**.6
    Millennium Development Goals **160**.32
male stereotyping as barrier to university entrance **139**.38
malnutrition *see* hunger
managers
    gender gap **154**.17
    gender pay gap **154**.38
    management style and workplace bullying **122**.29, 35

and workplace stress 100.18, 25
mania 125.19
manic depression *see* bipolar affective disorder
manufacturing sector employment 107.7, 10
marijuana *see* herbal cannabis
marine ecosystems, effect of climate change 151.9
marital status
    and population in England and Wales 106.26
    and remarriages 106.32
marker-assisted selection (MAS) 138.37-9
marker genes 138.4
market size, gambling industry 129.4
    National Lottery 129.9, 10
    online gambling 129.17, 19
marketing alcohol to young people 143.17
marriage
    age at 106.3, 25
    as an institution 106.5-6
    as a relationship 106.5-6
    arranged marriages 106.15, 15-18
    attitudes to 106.4-6, 11
    births outside 124.22
    changing views on 106.4-6, 20
    and Civil Partnerships 153.26
    'common law' marriages 106.8, 9-10
    early and forced marriage 120.29
    forced marriages 106.15; 155.16-18
    Government policies on 106.31
    and HIV/AIDS 96.24-5, 29, 34, 35
    inter-ethnic 115.25
    male and female attitudes to 106.6
    open marriages 106.18-19
    and premarital contracts 106.22-4
    remarriages 106.2, 3, 32
    statistics 106.2, 3
    and stepfamilies *see* stepfamilies
    and tax incentives 106.26
marriage counselling 106.27
mass mourning 116.17-18
massage 81.4
    and raising self-esteem 117.33
maternal health, Millennium Development Goals 160.31-2

maternal mortality 154.12
maternity leave 107.16, 21
mathematics, A-level performance 139.18
mature students 139.30, 32
maximum working hours 107.30-1
MDMA *see* ecstasy
means tested benefits 160.23, 24
meat consumption 88.6, 26, 31; 140.12-13, 15-18
    alternatives to meat 140.19, 26
    effects 140.13
    and fat 140.12
    game as food source 140.15, 17
    health issues 140.13, 21, 30
    illegal meat 88.39
    nutrients 140.12, 14
meat-eaters, and opposition to animal experiments 103.11
meat production
    effects of 140.13, 16-17
    organic 140.29-30
media
    accountability 142.17-30
    and body image 117.11-12, 15, 17-18; 127.23
        and eating disorders 127.25-6, 27
    breaking ethnic stereotypes 115.22
    control 142.1-16
    convergence 142.1-2
    and football-related violence 118.7
    government control 121.1
    government use of 121.17-18
    and health care information 117.18
    and homosexuality 153.23-5
    impact 142.31-9
    intrusion 142.23, 25, 26
    mergers 142.4
    negative representation of young people 137.24, 25
    over-reaction to terrorism 147.10-11
    ownership 121.4-5
    and people with learning difficulties 135.35
    portrayal of animal rights activists 103.11
    portrayal of disabled people 135.29, 32
    and pressure on athletes to use drugs 118.29
    and public perception of crime 137.2

Volume numbers appear first (in bold) followed by page numbers; a change in volume number is preceded by a semi-colon.

Vol. 74 Money Matters
Vol. 76 The Water Crisis
Vol. 78 Threatened Species
Vol. 81 Alternative Therapies
Vol. 82 Protecting our Privacy
Vol. 85 The Housing Crisis
Vol. 88 Food and Nutrition
Vol. 89 Refugees
Vol. 96 Preventing Sexual Diseases
Vol. 97 Energy Matters
Vol. 99 Exploited Children
Vol. 100 Stress and Anxiety
Vol. 103 Animal Rights
Vol. 106 Trends in Marriage
Vol. 107 Work Issues
Vol. 115 Racial Discrimination
Vol. 116 Grief and Loss
Vol. 117 Self-Esteem and Body Image
Vol. 118 Focus on Sport
Vol. 119 Transport Trends
Vol. 120 The Human Rights Issue
Vol. 121 The Censorship Debate

Vol. 122 Bullying
Vol. 123 Young People and Health
Vol. 124 Parenting Issues
Vol. 125 Understanding Depression
Vol. 126 The Abortion Debate
Vol. 127 Eating Disorders
Vol. 128 The Cannabis Issue
Vol. 129 Gambling Trends
Vol. 130 Homelessness
Vol. 131 Citizenship and National Identity
Vol. 132 Child Abuse
Vol. 133 Teen Pregnancy and Lone Parents
Vol. 134 Customers and Consumerism
Vol. 135 Coping with Disability
Vol. 136 Self-Harm
Vol. 137 Crime and Anti-Social Behaviour
Vol. 138 A Genetically Modified Future?
Vol. 139 The Education Problem
Vol. 140 Vegetarian and Vegan Diets
Vol. 141 Mental Health
Vol. 142 Media Issues
Vol. 143 Problem Drinking

Vol. 144 The Cloning Debate
Vol. 145 Smoking Trends
Vol. 146 Sustainability and Environment
Vol. 147 The Terrorism Problem
Vol. 148 Religious Beliefs
Vol. 149 A Classless Society?
Vol. 150 Migration and Population
Vol. 151 Climate Change
Vol. 152 Euthanasia and the Right to Die
Vol. 153 Sexual Orientation and Society
Vol. 154 The Gender Gap
Vol. 155 Domestic Abuse
Vol. 156 Travel and Tourism
Vol. 157 The Problem of Globalisation
Vol. 158 The Internet Revolution
Vol. 159 An Ageing Population
Vol. 160 Poverty and Exclusion
Vol. 161 Waste Issues
Vol. 162 Staying Fit
Vol. 163 Drugs in the UK

and suicide **136**.37-9
teenage magazines **142**.28
violence *see* violence, media
women in the media **154**.11
and women's sport **118**.21-2
mediation
and divorce **106**.38-9
and homelessness prevention **130**.30
medical abortion ('the abortion pill') **126**.10, 14, 32-4
medical benefits, GM crops **138**.9-10
medical model of disability **135**.1
medical profession
attitudes to euthanasia **152**.7, 8, 24-6, 27-8
effects of legalising euthanasia **152**.7
medical research and animal experimentation **140**.32-3; **144**.34
medical technology
and animal experiments **103**.10-11
medical tourism **156**.4-5
medical treatment
and the Mental Capacity Act **152**.37, 38
for obesity **162**.2-3, 6
patient's right to refuse **152**.2, 10-11
premature babies **152**.4, 32, 34
withdrawing or withholding **152**.3, 5-6
medical waste disposal **161**.24
medically-assisted dying *see* physician-assisted suicide
medicinal drug use **163**.1
cannabis **128**.4, 28, 36, 37
and the law **128**.37
multiple sclerosis **128**.36, 37
medicines
and alcohol **143**.10
animal testing of **103**.1, 11, 12-14
drug development **103**.2-3, 9, 10, 11, 13
and banned substances in sport **118**.32-3
from GM crops (pharming) **138**.4, 9-10, 20-22
memorial services **116**.17
memories of the deceased *see* remembrance of the deceased
memory, effect of cannabis use **128**.4-5
men
and abortion
involvement in decision-making **126**.13, 15-16
rights **126**.15
and alcohol
alcohol consumption **143**.8, 31
safe limits **143**.26, 34
attitudes **154**.16
body image and the media **117**.12
and compulsive shopping **134**.14
and depression **125**.13-15
and divorce **106**.31
and domestic violence **155**.12-13
and eating disorders **127**.3
fertility and smoking **145**.32
gender stereotypes **154**.7-8
homosexual activity **133**.2
and mental ill-health **141**.1
and online shopping **134**.16
and self-harm **136**.2
and sexual health **96**.13
single **106**.3, 12, 20

and smoking **145**.21, 22
and stress **100**.13, 19
and suicide **136**.33, 35, 36
meningitis **123**.5
Mental Capacity Act
and advance directives **152**.37
and doctors' right to end life **152**.38
mental health **141**.2, 34-6
and abortion **126**.11
and adolescents **123**.9
assessment after attempted suicide **136**.28
benefits of exercise **141**.34, 39; **162**.37, 38
and cannabis **128**.5, 8, 14-15; **163**.35
children **141**.37
and diet **125**.11-12; **141**.30-31, 34
and disability **135**.4
and domestic violence **155**.5
education in **141**.37
and homeless people **130**.11, 20, 27
and older people **159**.4
and smoking **145**.38-9
statistics **125**.16
and terrorism threat **147**.12
and workplace stress **100**.17-18, 20
and youth crime **137**.13
Mental Health Act 2007 **141**.26
mental illness
attitudes to **141**.25, 27
and cannabis **163**.35
children **141**.1, 20-21
and criminal behaviour **141**.2, 22
definition **141**.1
and eating disorders **127**.9-10
genetic predisposition to **141**.24
help for people with **141**.34-6
and homelessness **130**.11, 20, 27
and homosexuality **153**.3, 6
and medical research **103**.12
and poverty **141**.2, 22
prevalence **141**.1
mental symptoms of workplace bullying **122**.31
mental toughness and resisting bullying **122**.38
mentalities **149**.6
mercy killing (non-voluntary euthanasia) **152**.1, 3
mesomorph body shape **127**.22
metabolism **88**.15
effect of smoking **145**.26, 30-31
metals recycling **161**.24
aluminium **161**.22, 27
methamphetamine (crystal meth) **163**.16-17, 32
methane
emissions from agriculture **151**.7
trapping **151**.36
methyl alcohol (meths) **143**.1-2
MI5 (Security Service) **147**.2
MI6 (Secret Intelligence Service) **147**.2
mice
and creation of embryonic stem cells **144**.26
with human gene material **144**.11
microbes **88**.27, 28-9
microbicides **96**.34, 35

microgeneration of energy **151**.39

Microsoft
 and Chinese censorship **121**.19
 touch screen controls **158**.22-3
 Workability initiative (disability) **135**.15

middle-classes **149**.19-20
 children as bullies **122**.9-10
 residential mobility **149**.26
 and university application discrimination **149**.7

Mifepristone (the abortion pill) **126**.10, 14, 32-4

migrant workers
 exploitation **120**.30-31; **150**.14, 15, 19, 20, 22
 need for **150**.11
 UK **150**.4-5

migrants
 attitudes to **150**.3, 13-14, 17, 18-19
 and crime **150**.12, 13
 definition **150**.21
 and economic growth **150**.11, 17
 and sexual health **150**.21-3

migration **150**.1-27, 35
 data collection **150**.5
 definition **150**.4, 21
 effect on environment **150**.26-7
 global trends **150**.1-2
 lack of accurate data **150**.6, 19, 23
 and population growth, UK **85**.29, 30
 reasons for **150**.21, 24-5
 statistics **150**.4, 8-9, 23, 26, 35
 and unemployment **150**.9-10

military personnel, suicides, Japan **136**.39

milk
 from cloned cows **144**.36-8, 39
 vegetarian alternatives **140**.22, 26

Millennium Declaration **120**.3

Millennium Development Goals **160**.26, 28, 20-32
 and gender discrimination **154**.14
 and sustainable development **146**.1-2

minerals and vegetarian diets **140**.3

minicabs and disabled people **135**.9

minimum income standard **160**.8

minimum wage **107**.31

ministers of religion **148**.1

minority ethnic groups *see* ethnic minorities

miscegenation *see* mixed-race relationships

Misuse of Drugs Act **163**.2, 33

mitochondrial DNA **144**.17

mixed-faith relationships **115**.39

mixed-race families **124**.36-7

mixed-race people, Britain **115**.24-5
 as victims of crime **115**.10

mixed-race relationships **115**.22-3, 24-5

MNCs *see* (multi-national corporations)

mobile phones
 bullying by **122**.19, 21-5
 concerns about **158**.12, 32
 and gambling **129**.18, 26
 household ownership **134**.5
 and social networking **158**.11-12
 tracking of **82**.19-20
 usage trends **158**.4-5; 11-14

mobility component, Disability Living Allowance **135**.5

mock elections for young people **131**.27

models of disability **135**.1

Modern Apprenticeships **107**.36

Mohammed, Danish cartoons of **121**.10-13, 15-16; **142**.34

money
 attitudes to, and social class **149**.19-20
 and the cashless society **74**.9-11
 and children **74**.4, 5-6, 6-7, 12-13
 financial abuse **159**.16
 financial planning **74**.14-39
 students **74**.1, 17, 19-22, 28-32, 34-9
 worries
  non-traditional families **124**.20
  young people **123**.3

monoamine oxidase inhibitors (MAOIs) **125**.32

monogamy, and marriage **106**.18-19

mood and effects of alcohol **143**.7

mood stabilising drugs **125**.19, 25

moral decisions and humanism **148**.14-16

moral decline, Britain **148**.17

morning after pill (emergency contraception) **126**.24

morphine **152**.26-7

Volume numbers appear first (in bold) followed by page numbers; a change in volume number is preceded by a semi-colon.

Vol. **74** Money Matters
Vol. **76** The Water Crisis
Vol. **78** Threatened Species
Vol. **81** Alternative Therapies
Vol. **82** Protecting our Privacy
Vol. **85** The Housing Crisis
Vol. **88** Food and Nutrition
Vol. **89** Refugees
Vol. **96** Preventing Sexual Diseases
Vol. **97** Energy Matters
Vol. **99** Exploited Children
Vol. **100** Stress and Anxiety
Vol. **103** Animal Rights
Vol. **106** Trends in Marriage
Vol. **107** Work Issues
Vol. **115** Racial Discrimination
Vol. **116** Grief and Loss
Vol. **117** Self-Esteem and Body Image
Vol. **118** Focus on Sport
Vol. **119** Transport Trends
Vol. **120** The Human Rights Issue
Vol. **121** The Censorship Debate

Vol. **122** Bullying
Vol. **123** Young People and Health
Vol. **124** Parenting Issues
Vol. **125** Understanding Depression
Vol. **126** The Abortion Debate
Vol. **127** Eating Disorders
Vol. **128** The Cannabis Issue
Vol. **129** Gambling Trends
Vol. **130** Homelessness
Vol. **131** Citizenship and National Identity
Vol. **132** Child Abuse
Vol. **133** Teen Pregnancy and Lone Parents
Vol. **134** Customers and Consumerism
Vol. **135** Coping with Disability
Vol. **136** Self-Harm
Vol. **137** Crime and Anti-Social Behaviour
Vol. **138** A Genetically Modified Future?
Vol. **139** The Education Problem
Vol. **140** Vegetarian and Vegan Diets
Vol. **141** Mental Health
Vol. **142** Media Issues
Vol. **143** Problem Drinking

Vol. **144** The Cloning Debate
Vol. **145** Smoking Trends
Vol. **146** Sustainability and Environment
Vol. **147** The Terrorism Problem
Vol. **148** Religious Beliefs
Vol. **149** A Classless Society?
Vol. **150** Migration and Population
Vol. **151** Climate Change
Vol. **152** Euthanasia and the Right to Die
Vol. **153** Sexual Orientation and Society
Vol. **154** The Gender Gap
Vol. **155** Domestic Abuse
Vol. **156** Travel and Tourism
Vol. **157** The Problem of Globalisation
Vol. **158** The Internet Revolution
Vol. **159** An Ageing Population
Vol. **160** Poverty and Exclusion
Vol. **161** Waste Issues
Vol. **162** Staying Fit
Vol. **163** Drugs in the UK

mortality rates **150**.32
mortgages
    and first-time buyers **85**.6, 7
    help for lone parents **133**.34
    and interest rates **85**.6
    mortgage lending **134**.25
    and single people **85**.7
Mosaic profiling system **149**.17
    education and social class **149**.32
mosques
    improving governance standards **147**.34
    teaching in British mosques **147**.17-18
mothers
    employment patterns **107**.26; **149**.28; **154**.29
    full-time **124**.12
    identity confusion **149**.4-5
    and poverty **160**.15
    share of household tasks **124**.11
motor neurone disease (MND) and stem cell research **144**.32-3
motoring
    costs **119**.14
    and disability **135**.7
    spending on **134**.4, 25
    trends **119**.7-9
multiculturalism
    Britain **156**.11
    British Muslims support for **115**.34
    as hindrance to British identity **131**.10
    London **115**.23
multi-faith schools **148**.32-3
multi-infarct dementia (vascular dementia) **141**.6
multinational corporations (MNCs) **157**.6, 11
    and anti-globalisation campaigners **157**.30-31
    employment **157**.13
multinational water corporations, and the privatisation of water supplies **76**.22, 23, 29-30
multiple personality disorder **141**.12
multiple sclerosis (MS)
    and complementary medicine **81**.30-1
    and depression **125**.5
    and the medicinal use of cannabis **128**.36, 37
multiracial families **124**.36-7
multiracialism, Britain **115**.3, 23, 24-5, 38
multisensory alarms in cars **119**.19
mumps **123**.4-5
murder, bereavement by **116**.8
muscle dysmorphia **127**.19
music
    and mental health **141**.36
    and raising self-esteem **117**.33
Muslims
    British, feelings of identity **131**.9
    fears after London bombings **115**.36
    support for integration **115**.34
    young Muslims and fundamentalism **147**.16-17

nalbuphine hydrochloride **118**.35
nalmefene **129**.39

name changing
    and children's rights **120**.11
    and civil partnerships **153**.28
names for racial identity **115**.4-5
nandrolone precursors **118**.35
nappies, waste disposal **161**.1 5, 29
narcotic analgesics **118**.38
National Curriculum **139**.1-2, 5-6
    and alcohol education **143**.20
    pupils opinions **139**.7
    and specialist diplomas **139**.25
national identity **131**.1-14
    cards *see* identity cards
    effect of devolution **131**.6
    and ethnic groups **131**.8
    non-white ethnic groups **115**.38
    register **120**.35
National Lottery **129**.9-13
    good causes **129**.9
    Olympic Games funding **129**.9
    online, and under 16s **129**.12-13
    and social mobility **149**.22
    and under 16s **129**.11-13
national origin as grounds for discrimination **115**.7
nationalist-separatist terrorism **147**.1
nationality as grounds for discrimination **115**.7
natural burial **134**.31
natural cloning **144**.1
natural gas vehicles **119**.20-21
natural medicine *see* complementary medicine (CM)
natural resources **146**.9
nature and mental wellbeing **117**.38-9
naturopathy **81**.2, 19
needs, children **120**.2
negative body image see body image, negative
negative discipline **132**.18
negative experiences, learning from **117**.6
negative representation of young people **137**.24, 25
negative resource transfers **157**.7
negative thinking and low self-esteem **117**.6
neglect
    children **132**.1-2, 4-5
    and older people **159**.17
nervous system diseases and depression **125**.5
net neutrality **158**.24
neurobiology and gambling **129**.6
neurosis **141**.1
neurotransmitters **141**.9
news
    attitudes to **142**.31-3
    being interviewed **142**.11-12
    effect of media ownership **142**.5
    sources **142**.33
    women in news media **154**.11
news manipulation **121**.6
newspapers **142**.8-9
    advertising **134**.8
    cartoons of Mohammed **121**.10-13, 15-16; **142**.34
    and Freedom of Information Act **142**.17
    mergers **142**.4
    ownership **121**.4-5

readership **142**.8

sales **142**.9

as source of news **142**.33

NGOs *see* non-governmental organisations)

NHS (National Health Service)

and abortion **126**.12, 24

and complementary medicine **81**.4, 21

costs of **81**.31

effectiveness of **81**.22

funding **81**.27, 29, 36

and multiple sclerosis **81**.30-1

osteopathy **81**.7

reflexology **81**.17, 31

support for **81**.30-1

and eating disorders **127**.28

and HIV treatments **96**.21, 22

nicotine

addiction **145**.25-7, 35

chemical content **145**.25

children **145**.2-3

effects on the body **145**.25-6

gum **145**.37

inhalator **145**.37

nasal spray **145**.37

patches **145**.37

and young people **145**.20

replacement therapy **145**.33, 37

toxicity **145**.27

withdrawal symptoms **145**.26-7

night eating syndrome **127**.17-18

night shelters **130**.31

nitrogen oxide (NOx) emissions **146**.35

agriculture **151**.7

transport **119**.15, 16

no-blame policy and bullying **122**.12

no-earner families **149**.28

no-torture agreements and deportation **120**.38

non-contributory benefits **160**.23

non-governmental organisations (NGOs) **157**.7

and global water supplies **76**.30, 31

non-maintained special schools **135**.36

non-means tested benefits **160**.23

non-reproductive cloning *see* therapeutic cloning

non-traditional families **124**.20-21

non-traditional jobs for women **154**.31-2

non-violent direct action **121**.14

non-voluntary euthanasia **152**.1, 3

nose operations, and self-esteem **117**.27

nuclear power **97**.3-4, 19-23; **151**.29

building new power stations **97**.21-2

and clean-up of nuclear weapons material **97**.23

and climate change **97**.19-20, 21, 22

costs of **97**.6

debate over **97**.7

disadvantages of **97**.2, 7, 8

and electricity generation **97**.3-4, 22-3

environmental issues surrounding **97**.2, 4

and nuclear waste **97**.20, 22, 23

and radioactive discharges **97**.20

and renewable energy **97**.6, 7, 19, 21

and terrorism **97**.20

numbness

and traumatic bereavement **116**.10

numeracy problems, employees **139**.17

nurses, migration from developing countries **150**.15

nutrition

and ageing **159**.2

and meat **140**.12, 14

and mental health **141**.30-31, 34

teenagers **123**.6-7

vegetarians **140**.3-4, 6, 11

nutritional supplements **118**.28

and anti-doping rules **118**.33

NVQs (National Vocational Qualifications) **139**.4

obesity **88**.4, 9-11; **127**.32-9; **162**.1-10

avoidance *see* weight management

and Body Mass Index (BMI) **162**.1, 4, 5, 23

causes **162**.2, 5, 8

in children *see* childhood obesity

definitions **127**.33; **162**.1, 4

Volume numbers appear first (in bold) followed by page numbers; a change in volume number is preceded by a semi-colon.

Vol. **74** Money Matters

Vol. **76** The Water Crisis

Vol. **78** Threatened Species

Vol. **81** Alternative Therapies

Vol. **82** Protecting our Privacy

Vol. **85** The Housing Crisis

Vol. **88** Food and Nutrition

Vol. **89** Refugees

Vol. **96** Preventing Sexual Diseases

Vol. **97** Energy Matters

Vol. **99** Exploited Children

Vol. **100** Stress and Anxiety

Vol. **103** Animal Rights

Vol. **106** Trends in Marriage

Vol. **107** Work Issues

Vol. **115** Racial Discrimination

Vol. **116** Grief and Loss

Vol. **117** Self-Esteem and Body Image

Vol. **118** Focus on Sport

Vol. **119** Transport Trends

Vol. **120** The Human Rights Issue

Vol. **121** The Censorship Debate

Vol. **122** Bullying

Vol. **123** Young People and Health

Vol. **124** Parenting Issues

Vol. **125** Understanding Depression

Vol. **126** The Abortion Debate

Vol. **127** Eating Disorders

Vol. **128** The Cannabis Issue

Vol. **129** Gambling Trends

Vol. **130** Homelessness

Vol. **131** Citizenship and National Identity

Vol. **132** Child Abuse

Vol. **133** Teen Pregnancy and Lone Parents

Vol. **134** Customers and Consumerism

Vol. **135** Coping with Disability

Vol. **136** Self-Harm

Vol. **137** Crime and Anti-Social Behaviour

Vol. **138** A Genetically Modified Future?

Vol. **139** The Education Problem

Vol. **140** Vegetarian and Vegan Diets

Vol. **141** Mental Health

Vol. **142** Media Issues

Vol. **143** Problem Drinking

Vol. **144** The Cloning Debate

Vol. **145** Smoking Trends

Vol. **146** Sustainability and Environment

Vol. **147** The Terrorism Problem

Vol. **148** Religious Beliefs

Vol. **149** A Classless Society?

Vol. **150** Migration and Population

Vol. **151** Climate Change

Vol. **152** Euthanasia and the Right to Die

Vol. **153** Sexual Orientation and Society

Vol. **154** The Gender Gap

Vol. **155** Domestic Abuse

Vol. **156** Travel and Tourism

Vol. **157** The Problem of Globalisation

Vol. **158** The Internet Revolution

Vol. **159** An Ageing Population

Vol. **160** Poverty and Exclusion

Vol. **161** Waste Issues

Vol. **162** Staying Fit

Vol. **163** Drugs in the UK

discrimination **162**.21
economic costs **88**.4; **127**.33-4, 37
and genetics **127**.35
government strategies **162**.4-5, 9-10, 17-18, 22-3
and health **127**.32, 34; **162**.1-2, 5, 6, 7, 19, 25
measurement **162**.1
  children **127**. 36, 37
predictions **162**.10, 18, 19
statistics **127**.32, 33, 34; **162**.1, 5, 6, 7, 18
treatment **162**.2-3, 6, 20
in the workplace **162**.21
worldwide **162**.7
and young people **123**.31
obestatin (appetite-suppressing hormone) **127**.38-9
obsessions **141**.17
obsessive compulsive disorder (OCD) **141**.17
occupational choice, women **154**.30
  non-traditional **154**.31-2
occupational social class **149**.21
offender management bill **137**.30
offending and mental health problems **125**.16
offensive language, television **121**.38-9
official debt **157**.7
offsetting carbon **151**.20-22, 33-5
offshore wind farms **97**.12, 16, 26
offshoring **157**.35-6
oil
  depletion of resources **97**.8, 10
  leakages **97**.3
  recycling **161**.5, 23, 28
  and renewable energy **97**.10
older people
  abuse of **159**.4, 6, 16-18
  as carers **159**.4, 5
  and depression **125**.22-3
  excessive drinking **143**.9-10, 30
  and health **159**.4, 6, 8, 35-9
  and homelessness **130**.17-18
  in employment **159**.10, 15
  media consumption **158**.4
  and mental health problems **125**.16; **141**.2
  and self-harm **136**.20
  spending **159**.19
  worldwide **159**.5, 6
  UK **159**.3-4, 7-8
older workers **107**.12-13; **159**.10, 15
  and age discrimination **159**.4, 8-13
omega 3 fatty acids
  and attention-deficit hyperactivity disorder **141**.19
  in eggs **140**.39
  in meat **140**.12, 21
one-parent families *see* lone parents
one planet economy **146**.8
online brands **142**.35
online bullying **122**.19-26
online child abuse **132**.33
  images **132**.31-2
online crime **158**.3, 33-4, 35, 36
online dating scams **134**.27
online entertainments **158**.21-2
online fraud **134**.26-9

online gambling **129**.17-18, 19-25
  and addiction **129**.21-2
  National Lottery games and under 16s **129**.12-13
  participation rates **129**.17, 19
  poker, underage **129**.25
  at work **129**.22-4
online gaming addiction **158**.39
online grooming **132**.33
online journalism register **142**.16
online learning **139**.28
online reporting of crime **137**.31
online retail *see* Internet shopping
online terrorism **147**.8-9
online travel booking **156**.1, 13, 14; **158**.3
open marriages **106**.18-19
opiates/opioids **163**.5, 25
opium production **163**.25
Oregon State, euthanasia **152**.4, 18, 19, 31, 33
organ donation **116**.31
organ transplants *see* therapeutic cloning
organic farming **146**.25, 27
  animal welfare **140**.35-6
  meat production **140**.29-30
  unable to meet demand for food **140**.36-7
organic food **88**.13-14, 18, 33, 34
  and Fairtrade **134**.37
organic shops **134**.30, 31
organic waste, composting **161**.19, 28-9, 30
organized crime bill **137**.30
orthorexia nervosa **127**.19
osteopathy **81**.6-7, 23, 36
osteoporosis and chiropractic **81**.9
ostrich farming **140**.30
out-of-school learning **139**.27-8
outdoor activities
  and interfaith relations **148**.31
  and mental well-being **117**.38-9
outdoor (released) GMOs **138**.12
outreach teams for homeless people **130**.31
overdoses *see* drug overdoses
overdrafts **134**.22, 24
overgeneralisation and low self-esteem **117**.6
overseas students **139**.30, 31, 32
overseas travel trends **119**.1; **156**.1-2, 4-5
overseas visitors to UK **156**.3-4, 10, 13
overseas workers, UK dependence on **146**.6
overweight people **127**.32, 33
  children **119**.31
overworking **154**.18
ownership of the media **121**.4-5
  effect on news **142**.5
  mergers **142**.4
  newspapers **142**.9
ozone and air pollution **146**.35
ozone layer depletion **151**.4

P

packaging waste **161**.4, 5, 12
paedophiles **132**.22

help for **132**.36-9
paedophobia (fear of young people) **137**.26-7
pain
absence during self-harm **136**.1
definition **152**.2
pain relief
and acupuncture **81**.5
painkillers, misuse **163**.14-15
paint, disposal of **161**.23
palliative care **152**.1-2, 5, 9, 22, 27
effect of legalising euthanasia **152**.4
limits of **152**.10
pancreas repair, stem cell therapy **144**.21
panic attacks after bereavement **116**.4
paper **161**.5, 22
recycling **161**.24, 26
paranoia **141**.5
parasuicide **123**.36; **136**.24
Parental Guidance (PG) classification **121**.29
parental leave **107**.21
parental responsibility **124**.4; **133**.39; **153**.33
parental rights **153**.33-4
parenting **124**.1-19
styles **124**.8
parents
absence due to divorce, effect on children **124**.34
and adult children **124**.3, 14-15
and alcohol
alcohol abuse **143**.37
influence on young people **143**.5, 17
authoritarian **124**.8
authoritative **124**.8
awareness of mobile bullying **122**.25
of bullies **122**.8-9
celebrity role models **124**.6
and child labour **99**.3
and children as consumers **134**.12
and children's participation **120**.10
and children's television viewing **121**.26, 27, 32
and children's video game use **121**.32-3
cohabiting and married **106**.21-2
death of **116**.12-13

disciplining children **132**.18
discussing eating disorders **127**.25
divorcing **106**.33-8
education as factor in university application **149**.7, 31
and exam stress **123**.30
fathers' rights and responsibilities
fears over child safety **124**.13-14
feelings of failure **124**.16-17
homosexual **153**.20-22
of lesbians and gay people **153**.9-10
with mental health problems **141**.24-5
and mobile phone tracking **82**.20
and money matters
savings **74**.7
teaching children about **74**.1, 5-6
non-traditional families **124**.20-21
parenting skills **124**.2
parenting styles **124**.8; **132**.18
permissive **124**.8
and pregnant teenagers **126**.28, 29
protection of children **137**.20
responsibilities **124**.4, 5; **133**.39
rights **133**.39
and self-harm by children **136**.14
sex education involvement **133**.12, 15
and smacking **132**.8-11, 15-16, 17
smoking, effects on children **145**.2, 32-3
and stress **100**.13
and student finance **74**.19, 38; **139**.34, 35
support for **120**.13; **124**.5, 6, 16-17
supporting adult children **124**.3
of teenagers **124**.16-17
time spent with children **106**.2
unmarried **124**.22
parking
concessions for disabled people **135**.7-8
illegal **119**.9
Parkinson's disease
and dementia **141**.6
and depression **125**.5
Parliament **131**.15
women in **154**.4, 6, 12

Volume numbers appear first (in bold) followed by page numbers; a change in volume number is preceded by a semi-colon.

Vol. **74** Money Matters
Vol. **76** The Water Crisis
Vol. **78** Threatened Species
Vol. **81** Alternative Therapies
Vol. **82** Protecting our Privacy
Vol. **85** The Housing Crisis
Vol. **88** Food and Nutrition
Vol. **89** Refugees
Vol. **96** Preventing Sexual Diseases
Vol. **97** Energy Matters
Vol. **99** Exploited Children
Vol. **100** Stress and Anxiety
Vol. **103** Animal Rights
Vol. **106** Trends in Marriage
Vol. **107** Work Issues
Vol. **115** Racial Discrimination
Vol. **116** Grief and Loss
Vol. **117** Self-Esteem and Body Image
Vol. **118** Focus on Sport
Vol. **119** Transport Trends
Vol. **120** The Human Rights Issue
Vol. **121** The Censorship Debate

Vol. **122** Bullying
Vol. **123** Young People and Health
Vol. **124** Parenting Issues
Vol. **125** Understanding Depression
Vol. **126** The Abortion Debate
Vol. **127** Eating Disorders
Vol. **128** The Cannabis Issue
Vol. **129** Gambling Trends
Vol. **130** Homelessness
Vol. **131** Citizenship and National Identity
Vol. **132** Child Abuse
Vol. **133** Teen Pregnancy and Lone Parents
Vol. **134** Customers and Consumerism
Vol. **135** Coping with Disability
Vol. **136** Self-Harm
Vol. **137** Crime and Anti-Social Behaviour
Vol. **138** A Genetically Modified Future?
Vol. **139** The Education Problem
Vol. **140** Vegetarian and Vegan Diets
Vol. **141** Mental Health
Vol. **142** Media Issues
Vol. **143** Problem Drinking

Vol. **144** The Cloning Debate
Vol. **145** Smoking Trends
Vol. **146** Sustainability and Environment
Vol. **147** The Terrorism Problem
Vol. **148** Religious Beliefs
Vol. **149** A Classless Society?
Vol. **150** Migration and Population
Vol. **151** Climate Change
Vol. **152** Euthanasia and the Right to Die
Vol. **153** Sexual Orientation and Society
Vol. **154** The Gender Gap
Vol. **155** Domestic Abuse
Vol. **156** Travel and Tourism
Vol. **157** The Problem of Globalisation
Vol. **158** The Internet Revolution
Vol. **159** An Ageing Population
Vol. **160** Poverty and Exclusion
Vol. **161** Waste Issues
Vol. **162** Staying Fit
Vol. **163** Drugs in the UK

part-time jobs **107**.17, 18, 19, 22
    children and teenagers with **74**.6, 8, 9
    and the pay gap **154**.6, 36
    and students **74**.20, 37; **139**.35
participation rights, children **120**.9-11
participation in sport **118**.9
    adults **118**.1
    female **118**.18-20
    school team sports **118**.4
    young people **118**.2; **123**.2
        long term benefits **137**.26
particulates emissions **119**.15
parties and alcohol **123**.17
parties, political *see* political parties
passive euthanasia **152**.5
passive smoking **145**.2, 28-9
    effect on children **123**.12; **145**.2, 28-9
passports **89**.33
    and identity cards **82**.9-10, 12
patents **138**.4
    genes **138**.23
paternity leave **107**.21
pathological gambling *see* compulsive gambling
patient confidentiality *see* confidentiality
Patients (Assisted Dying) Bill **152**.1, 29
patients' rights to refuse treatment **152**.2, 10-11
pay gap *see* gender pay gap
PE in schools **118**.3
peaceful protesting **121**.14
pedestrians and road accidents **119**.5, 30-31
peer pressure
    on athletes to use drugs **118**.29
    and children's food choices **123**.32
    and drinking behaviour **143**.17
    and drug use **128**.10
    and sexual intercourse **123**.21
    and smoking **145**.4
peer support
    and bullying **122**.12
    and self-harm **136**.8, 16, 18
peer-to-peer (P2P) downloading **158**.36
PEGI game classification system **121**.33
penal system, prohibition of corporal punishment **132**.15
penalties
    cannabis cultivation **128**.31
    cannabis supply **128**.2, 9, 13
    drink-driving **143**.24
    for drug smuggling **163**.38
    possession of cannabis **128**.2, 9, 13, 27, 30, 31, 32
    underage sale of alcohol **143**.2
pensions **89**.23
    and civil partnerships **153**.28
    Europe **159**.25
    gender gap **154**.6
    saving for **134**.4, 25; **159**.21, 22
        graduates **139**.36
    UK **159**.3, 23, 25
    universal social pension **159**.24
    and young people **74**.1-2
peptide hormones and analogues **118**.37
permissive parenting style **124**.8

personal crime, racial identity of victims **115**.10
personal information, control of **158**.31-4
personal skills gap **149**.37-8
personality and depression susceptibility **125**.2
pesco-vegetarian diet **140**.2
pester power **134**.12
pesticides **88**.13, 32, 34, 35
    GM viruses **138**.13-14
petrol prices **119**.12-13, 14
pets, death of **116**.13-14
PG film classification **121**.29
pharmaceutical industry **163**.1
    and animal experiments **103**.9, 12-14
    and herbal medicine **81**.11
pharming **138**.4, 9-10, 20-22
    hens for cancer treatment **138**.20-21
    rice **138**.20
    risks **138**.20, 21, 22
    tobacco plants for HIV treatment **138**.21-2
phishing **134**.27-8, 28-9; **158**.33-4
phobias **141**.16-17
    and young people **100**.2
phone bothering by parents **124**.15
phone-tapping in the workplace **120**.33
physical abuse
    of children **132**.1, **4**
    of older people **159**.16
    signs of **132**.4
    and stress **100**.1, 2
physical activity *see* exercise
physical punishment *see* corporal punishment
physical signs of bullying **122**.13, 30, 31
physician-assisted suicide (PAS) **152**.4, 7-8, 29-30, 31
phytochemicals **88**.5, 7, 13
pica **127**.17
Pick's disease **141**.7
Pilates **162**.34
pill, contraceptive **123**.23
    risk alert, impact on teenage pregnancy rate **126**.31
pink plateau **153**.39
pirate radio **142**.7
placebo effect, and complementary medicine **81**.26, 28, 34
plagiarism and the Internet **158**.2, 19-20
planning applications and sports facilities **118**.5
plants
    endangered species **78**.2-3, 7
    and photosynthesis **97**.9
    in tropical rainforests **78**.11
plasmids **138**.2
plastic bags **161**.5, 13-14, 19, 36-7
plastic surgery *see* cosmetic surgery
plastic waste **161**.5, 22, 29
    recycling **161**.24, 29
playground bullying and screen violence **121**.28
playgrounds for older people **159**.39
playing fields **118**.5-6
pocket money **74**.6, 8, 9, 13, 14
poisoning, first aid **136**.23
poker, online, and underage gambling **129**.25
police **137**.32-4
    arrest, your rights **128**.35-6

and asylum communities **89**.20
and beggars **130**.33
and child abuse **132**.3
Community Support Officers (CSO) **137**.33
concerns about migrant crime **150**.12
domestic violence units **155**.29
and drugs offences **163**.38
and football hooliganism **118**.8
and identity cards **82**.8
and instant justice **137**.34
and the law on hunting **103**.31
and online child pornography **99**.24
and racial discrimination **137**.32-3
recorded crime figures **137**.3
reporting a crime to **137**.30
and surveillance **82**.23
and Terrorism Act **147**.3
stop and search powers **147**.35-7
young people's opinions of **137**.14
political action and eating disorders **127**.26
political media, women in **154**.11
political and military globalisation **157**.2
political overreaction to terrorism **147**.10-11, 38-9
political parties **131**.18
young peoples's support **131**.32
political pressure on athletes **118**.29
politics
and competitive sport **118**.4
and crime **137**.1-2
and free speech **121**.7
and genomics **138**.3
and gender equality **154**.4, 6, 12, 21
and the media **142**.2
and newspapers **142**.8
older people's engagement in **159**.7
recommendations for change **131**.25
and support of media companies **121**.5
young people's involvement **131**.27-35
portage educational support **135**.36
postal voting **131**.16
pollution
from aviation **119**.16

and endangered species **78**.6
in the UK **78**.28, 29, 32
and species extinction **78**.11
and transport **119**.12, 13-14, 16, 30, 31; **146**.35-6
Poor Laws **149**.13
poorism (tourists visitng deprived areas) **156**.33-5
population **150**.28-39
ageing population **159**.3, 6
and development goals **150**.34
global trends **150**.34-5; **159**.6
information from census **150**.36
and poverty **150**.34
sustainable **150**.31-2
population changes
see ageing population; population growth
population control to combat climate change **151**.31-2
population density and refugees **89**.23
population growth **89**.31
and endangered species **78**.1
and the environment **146**.12-13, 16-17; **150**.27
global **150**.31, 32-3, 34
and global water shortages **76**.3, 5, 8, 15
and immigration **150**.16
and migration **85**.29, 30
and water consumption **76**.22, 29
UK **150**.28, 29, 31
population studies (epidemiology) **103**.17, 18, 19, 22
pornography
and the Internet **158**.3
R18 films **121**.25, 20
port policing strategy, anti-terrorism **147**.29
positive action and age discrimination **159**.9-10
positive body image **117**.10
positive discipline **132**.18
positive discrimination **154**.36
positive thinking **117**.2, 6; **141**.36
as help for depression **125**.3
possession of cannabis **128**.2, 9, 13, 27, 30, 31, 32
postcodes and population profiling **149**.17
post-compulsory education **139**.2
post-mortem examination **116**.32
post-natal depression **125**.4, 17-18

Volume numbers appear first (in bold) followed by page numbers; a change in volume number is preceded by a semi-colon.

Vol. 74 Money Matters
Vol. 76 The Water Crisis
Vol. 78 Threatened Species
Vol. 81 Alternative Therapies
Vol. 82 Protecting our Privacy
Vol. 85 The Housing Crisis
Vol. 88 Food and Nutrition
Vol. 89 Refugees
Vol. 96 Preventing Sexual Diseases
Vol. 97 Energy Matters
Vol. 99 Exploited Children
Vol. 100 Stress and Anxiety
Vol. 103 Animal Rights
Vol. 106 Trends in Marriage
Vol. 107 Work Issues
Vol. 115 Racial Discrimination
Vol. 116 Grief and Loss
Vol. 117 Self-Esteem and Body Image
Vol. 118 Focus on Sport
Vol. 119 Transport Trends
Vol. 120 The Human Rights Issue
Vol. 121 The Censorship Debate

Vol. 122 Bullying
Vol. 123 Young People and Health
Vol. 124 Parenting Issues
Vol. 125 Understanding Depression
Vol. 126 The Abortion Debate
Vol. 127 Eating Disorders
Vol. 128 The Cannabis Issue
Vol. 129 Gambling Trends
Vol. 130 Homelessness
Vol. 131 Citizenship and National Identity
Vol. 132 Child Abuse
Vol. 133 Teen Pregnancy and Lone Parents
Vol. 134 Customers and Consumerism
Vol. 135 Coping with Disability
Vol. 136 Self-Harm
Vol. 137 Crime and Anti-Social Behaviour
Vol. 138 A Genetically Modified Future?
Vol. 139 The Education Problem
Vol. 140 Vegetarian and Vegan Diets
Vol. 141 Mental Health
Vol. 142 Media Issues
Vol. 143 Problem Drinking

Vol. 144 The Cloning Debate
Vol. 145 Smoking Trends
Vol. 146 Sustainability and Environment
Vol. 147 The Terrorism Problem
Vol. 148 Religious Beliefs
Vol. 149 A Classless Society?
Vol. 150 Migration and Population
Vol. 151 Climate Change
Vol. 152 Euthanasia and the Right to Die
Vol. 153 Sexual Orientation and Society
Vol. 154 The Gender Gap
Vol. 155 Domestic Abuse
Vol. 156 Travel and Tourism
Vol. 157 The Problem of Globalisation
Vol. 158 The Internet Revolution
Vol. 159 An Ageing Population
Vol. 160 Poverty and Exclusion
Vol. 161 Waste Issues
Vol. 162 Staying Fit
Vol. 163 Drugs in the UK

diagnosis of **125**.17
symptoms of **125**.17
treatment for **125**.17-18
post-traumatic stress disorder (PTSD) **116**.10; **137**.29; **141**.3, 12
potatoes, GM research trials **138**.27, 28
poverty
    and affordable housing
        in rural areas **85**.5
    attitudes to **160**.3, 4
    causes of **160**.2, 25-6
    and child labour **99**.2, 3, 4, 14-15; **120**.19
    children living in *see* child poverty
    children's perceptions of **149**.9-12; **160**.4
    and debt **160**.12, 33
    definitions **160**.1, 25, 26
    and disabled people **135**.16-18; **160**.10
    and education **160**.16-22
    and environmental stress **146**.16-17
    experiences of **160**.13-14, 27
    extent of **160**.1-2
    and free trade **157**.9, 13, 26-7
    global **160**.25-39
    government action **160**.21-2
    and government debt **157**.9-10
    and health **149**.14; **160**.2
    and HIV/AIDS **96**.24, 29
    impact of **160**.2, 13-14
    measuring **160**.1, 8
    and mental health problems **141**.2, 22
    and Millennium Development Goals **160**.30
    and older people **159**.3
    and population **150**.34
    and post traumatic stress disorder **141**.3
    rich-poor gap
        global **160**.26, 29
        UK **115**.32; **149**.19, 20, 22, 27, 29; **160**.6, 7
    and segregation **115**.30, 31, 32
    and the sexual exploitation of children **99**.16, 24
    and smoking **145**.21
    statistics **160**.1-2, 25, 29
    and teenage pregnancy **133**.20, 21
    in the UK **160**.1-24
    and urbanization **150**.38
    and water
        and development aid **76**.30-1
        and human rights **76**.25
        multinational water corporations **76**.29
        supplies in developing countries **76**.6
    and women **160**.15
poverty line **160**.1
power gap **154**.4, 6
power and self-esteem **117**.4, 31-2
Prader-Willi Syndrome **127**.17
praise and self-esteem **117**.34
prayer **148**.1
pre-implantation genetic diagnosis **144**.20
pre-school children
    effects of divorce **124**.33
    gender differences **154**.24
    normal sexual behaviour **132**.29-30
    effects of poverty **160**.20

precursor cells **144**.25
pregnancy
    and alcohol **143**.3, 25, 27, 33-4
    development **126**.26
    and domestic violence **155**.11, 30
    and exercise **162**.32
    and HIV **96**.16, 22, 23, 31, 38
    and male depression **125**.14
    men's rights **126**.15
    planned, teenagers **133**.20
    and smoking **88**.7; **145**.32-3
    testing **133**.8
    unplanned, options **126**.9-10
prejudice
    against bisexuals **153**.10
    definition **115**.4
    in childhood, and low self-esteem **117**.32
    against disabled people **135**.15, 30-31
    fears of parents of gay children **153**.9
    Islamaphobia **115**.36
    racial **131**.2
    religious **131**.3
    and sexual orientation **153**.2
    against transgender people **153**.13
premature babies, treatment decisions **152**.4, 32, 34
prenuptial contracts **106**.22-4
prescription drugs, misuse **163**.14-16
press *see* media
Press Code **142**.26
press conferences **142**.12-13
pressure on athletes to use drugs **118**.29
prices
    alcohol, effect on consumption **143**.17, 31
    cannabis **128**.2, 6
    cigarettes **145**.17
        as deterrent to children smoking **145**.3
Primark and ethical trading **134**.30
primary age children, effects of divorce **124**.33
primary schools
    curriculum **139**.5, 6
    and gay issues **153**.19-20
    gender gap **154**.23
    and homophobic bullying **153**.15
    pupil behaviour **120**.16
    and pupils' mental health **141**.37
primate with jelly fish genes **144**.11
prisons **137**.37-9
    and children **120**.12
    corporal punishment prohibition **132**.15
    costs **137**.37
    prison leavers and homelessness **130**.11, 15
    prison population **137**.1, 37
        international comparisons **137**.38
    Prison Rules **137**.38
    prisoners' rights **137**.37-8
    private prisons **137**.2
    and self-harm **137**.37
    sentences for cannabis possession **128**.13
    and women **137**.39
privacy
    children's right to **120**.12

and the media **142**.25, 26

privacy enhancing technology (PET), and RFID tags **82**.16

privacy-invading software and domestic abuse **155**.15-16

privacy rights **82**.1-3, 39
    bodily privacy **82**.5
    and communications data **82**.1-2
    communications privacy **82**.5
    comprehensive laws on **82**.5
    defining privacy **82**.4
    and human rights **82**.4-5, 18
    information privacy **82**.5
    models of privacy protection **82**.5
    and RFID tags **82**.13-17, 35
    and technologies of privacy **82**.5
    viewpoints on privacy **82**.4
    in the workplace **82**.25-30

private communication interception **120**.34

private sales and consumer rights **134**.20

private schoolchildren
    attitudes to social differences **149**.9-12
    children's perceptions of **149**.11-12

private schools and university entrance **149**.34-5

privatisation
    and water management **76**.22-3, 32
        criticisms of private companies **76**.32
        multinational water corporations **76**.22, 23, 29-30

pro-abortion arguments **126**.21

pro-life arguments **126**.21-2

pro-life movement **126**.25
    and abortion time-limit **126**.38

problem debt **134**.23

problem drinking *see* alcohol abuse

problem gambling *see* compulsive gambling

production, sustainable **146**.7, 8

promoters, sports, pressure on athletes to use drugs **118**.29

propaganda, terrorist, online **147**.8

protection of children
    from abuse **120**.14-15
    refugees **120**.22

protectionism **157**.7, 13, 23-4

protectiveness, parental **124**.13-14

proteins **88**.6, 8

definition **138**.4

drugs produced by GM hens **138**.20-21

and vegan diet **140**.23-4

and vegetarian diet **140**.3, 7

PSHE (personal, social and health education) **133**.16

psoriasis and smoking **145**.30

psychedelic drugs **163**.2, 6

psychiatric patients and smoking **145**.38

psychic prediction scams **134**.26

psychological abuse of older people **159**.16

psychological bullying **122**.10

psychological conditions and eating disorders **127**.9-10

psychological damage caused by corporal punishment **132**.10

psychological dependency on cannabis **128**.8

psychological effects of nicotine **145**.26

psychological health requirements **117**.8

psychologists, and young people and stress **100**.2

psychology
    of class **149**.6
    and gambling **129**.6, 29
    and religion **148**.12-13

psychosis **141**.1
    cannabis use **128**.15

psychosurgery **125**.26

psychotherapy
    and bipolar disorder **141**.14-15
    as a treatment for depression **125**.7, 26, 33
    and young people and stress **100**.2

PTSD (post-traumatic stress disorder) **116**.10; **137**.29; **141**.3, 12

puberty **127**.22
    and eating disorders **127**.2, 22-4

public attitudes
    to biotechnology **138**.15-16; **144**.19
    to cannabis use **128**.12
    to film classification **121**.24
    to euthanasia **152**.8, 12, 13, 15, 17
    to genetic modification **138**.3; **144**.20
    to human cloning **144**.35
    to legal protection for gay people **153**.36
    to marriage and cohabitation **106**.4-6
    to mental ill-health **141**.25, 27
    to migrants **150**.3, 13-14, 17, 18-19

Volume numbers appear first (in bold) followed by page numbers; a change in volume number is preceded by a semi-colon.

Vol. **74** Money Matters
Vol. **76** The Water Crisis
Vol. **78** Threatened Species
Vol. **81** Alternative Therapies
Vol. **82** Protecting our Privacy
Vol. **85** The Housing Crisis
Vol. **88** Food and Nutrition
Vol. **89** Refugees
Vol. **96** Preventing Sexual Diseases
Vol. **97** Energy Matters
Vol. **99** Exploited Children
Vol. **100** Stress and Anxiety
Vol. **103** Animal Rights
Vol. **106** Trends in Marriage
Vol. **107** Work Issues
Vol. **115** Racial Discrimination
Vol. **116** Grief and Loss
Vol. **117** Self-Esteem and Body Image
Vol. **118** Focus on Sport
Vol. **119** Transport Trends
Vol. **120** The Human Rights Issue
Vol. **121** The Censorship Debate

Vol. **122** Bullying
Vol. **123** Young People and Health
Vol. **124** Parenting Issues
Vol. **125** Understanding Depression
Vol. **126** The Abortion Debate
Vol. **127** Eating Disorders
Vol. **128** The Cannabis Issue
Vol. **129** Gambling Trends
Vol. **130** Homelessness
Vol. **131** Citizenship and National Identity
Vol. **132** Child Abuse
Vol. **133** Teen Pregnancy and Lone Parents
Vol. **134** Customers and Consumerism
Vol. **135** Coping with Disability
Vol. **136** Self-Harm
Vol. **137** Crime and Anti-Social Behaviour
Vol. **138** A Genetically Modified Future?
Vol. **139** The Education Problem
Vol. **140** Vegetarian and Vegan Diets
Vol. **141** Mental Health
Vol. **142** Media Issues
Vol. **143** Problem Drinking

Vol. **144** The Cloning Debate
Vol. **145** Smoking Trends
Vol. **146** Sustainability and Environment
Vol. **147** The Terrorism Problem
Vol. **148** Religious Beliefs
Vol. **149** A Classless Society?
Vol. **150** Migration and Population
Vol. **151** Climate Change
Vol. **152** Euthanasia and the Right to Die
Vol. **153** Sexual Orientation and Society
Vol. **154** The Gender Gap
Vol. **155** Domestic Abuse
Vol. **156** Travel and Tourism
Vol. **157** The Problem of Globalisation
Vol. **158** The Internet Revolution
Vol. **159** An Ageing Population
Vol. **160** Poverty and Exclusion
Vol. **161** Waste Issues
Vol. **162** Staying Fit
Vol. **163** Drugs in the UK

to poverty **160**.3
to refugees **89**.17
to smacking **132**.8, 18
to smoking ban **145**.18
terrorism fears **147**.12
public grief **116**.17-18
public interest
and journalists' rights **142**.27
and media mergers **142**.4
public safety and censorship **121**.13
public service broadcasting, news coverage **142**.33
public services and gender equality **154**.3
public transport **119**.1, 12, 25
and disabled people **135**.8
encouraging use of **119**.39
usage **151**.39
pubs
and smoking ban **145**.13
and young people **143**.2
punishment
in schools, and racism **115**.19
pupils
behaviour **120**.16
opinions on National Curriculum **139**.7
pupil referral units **135**.36
pyramid selling **134**.26

qualifications **89**.34-5; **107**.1, 34; **139**.4
and ethnicity **139**.8
and gender **139**.10
for university entrance **139**.29-30
quality of goods, consumer rights **134**.2, 17
quitting smoking *see* smoking, giving up
quotas for migrant workers **150**.7
quotations and consumer rights **134**.18

R18 film classification **121**.25, 30
rabbit-human embryos **144**.11
race
and domestic violence **155**.4
definition **115**.4
as grounds for discrimination **115**.7
names for **115**.4-5
race hate trials **121**.15
race relations **147**.19
racial background, UK population **115**.3, 24-5
racial discrimination **115**.4, 7-8
and academic freedom **121**.8, 9
in employment **115**.13
racial equality in football **118**.15-16
racial harassment
defining **115**.8
of refugees **89**.19, 20
racial identity
confusion over **149**.4

victims of crime **115**.10
racial integration **107**.12; **115**.6, 28-9; **131**.9; **147**.19
Asians **115**.37
in education **115**.29, 33
racial profiling and 'stop and search' **147**.35-6
racial segregation **115**.28-32
racially motivated crime **115**.9-10
racism **115**.1-2, 4
challenging **115**.2
and ChildLine **115**.1
and children **115**.9
defining **115**.4
and education **115**.19-20
effects of **115**.1
in football **118**.14
and Islamophobia **115**.36
laws **115**.2, 7-8, 11-12, 26
perception of **131**.2
and the police **137**.32-3
reasons for **115**.1-2
in schools **115**.9, 19-20; **139**.9
in the workplace **115**.11-14
racist bullying **115**.2; **122**.4-5
racist incidents **115**.9
racist violence **137**.8, 16
radio **158**.5, 6
interviews **142**.13-14
as news source **142**.33
pirate stations **142**.7
railways
congestion **119**.35
and disabled people **135**.8
travel trends **119**.1; **161**.31-2
rainfall and water distribution in the UK **76**.1-2
rainforests *see* forestry
rape
number of reported rapes **137**.8
rate of return on education **139**.1, 37
re-offending rates, young offenders **137**.11, 15
reactive depression **125**.4
reality TV
breaking ethnic stereotypes **115**.22
and offensive language **121**.38-9
reclassification of cannabis **128**.13, 26-8, 29; **163**.32, 35-6
criticized **128**.38
effect on health **128**.30-32, 38
public attitudes to **128**.12
recombinant DNA technologies *see* genetic modification
recreational drug use **163**.1
recruitment of employees, discrimination **115**.13
recycling **161**.2, 18, 19, 22-9
employment in **161**.2
increase in **161**.31
mobile phones **158**.13
negative effects **161**.35
organic waste *see* composting waste
organisations **161**.9
in public places **161**.20, 21
reducing emissions **161**.3

statistics **161**.22

targets **161**.20

redress (compensation) **134**.2, 17

reduce, reuse, recycle **161**.7, 18

reducing waste **161**.18

incentives for **161**.38

reflexology **81**.3, 15-17, 23, 36

and stress-related illnesses **81**.16

training as a reflexologist **81**.16-17

refugees **120**.31

children **120**.21-2

and homelessness **130**.11-12, 19

refuges **155**.12-13, 27-8, 32-3

regional differences

disability **135**.2

smoking **145**.1, 21

social class **149**.18

register of domestic violence offenders **155**.39

register of GM land **138**.19, 36

registering a death **116**.31

regulation

of children's viewing **121**.26-7

of cloning **144**.3

of genetic modification **138**.3, 11

film **121**.22-5, 29-30

of hybrid embryo research **144**.14

media

and civil liberties **142**.1-2

mergers **142**.4

online journalism **142**.16

stem cell cloning **144**.27-8

television **121**.36-7

video **121**.26, 31

video games **121**.32-3

relationship support **106**.29-30

relationships

breakdown, and homelessness **130**.3, 11, 15

and cannabis use **128**.9

and depression, men **125**.14

and football supporting **141**.33

and human cloning **144**.6

and mental health **141**.34

mixed-faith **115**.39

mixed-race **115**.22-5

and mobile phones **158**.13

relaxation

and depression **125**.39

and self-esteem **117**.35, 37

and stress **100**.29-30, 31-2, 34, 36-7

released (outdoor) GMOs **138**.12

relief, feelings after bereavement **116**.4, 19

religion **148**.1-39

and abortion **126**.1-3, 6

attitudes to **148**.26, 27

and the Census (2001) **148**.6-7

and children's rights **120**.2

and corporal punishment **132**.11

and euthanasia **152**.7, 11, 12, 15, 34

and food rules **148**.10-11

functions **148**.1

funeral traditions **116**.33-5

and the law **148**.29

and moral decline **148**.17

religious observance in Britain **148**.6-8, 18-19, 25, 27

religious tolerance **148**.23-39

surveys **148**.8, 27

and terrorism **147**.1

theories of **148**.12-13

women in the workforce **154**.29

religious discrimination **115**.26; **148**.28, 29

religious groups

and disability **135**.2

segregation **115**.32

religious identity **115**.5, 26

religious prejudice, perception of **131**.3

religiously motivated crime **115**.27; **137**.16; **148**.29

terrorism **147**.1, 5

religious texts **148**.1

religious values **148**.16

remembrance of the deceased **116**.16-17, 20, 24

remembrance book **116**.16

remembrance ceremonies **116**.23

remembrance services **116**.17

remittances from migrants **150**.2

Volume numbers appear first (in bold) followed by page numbers; a change in volume number is preceded by a semi-colon.

Vol. **74** Money Matters

Vol. **76** The Water Crisis

Vol. **78** Threatened Species

Vol. **81** Alternative Therapies

Vol. **82** Protecting our Privacy

Vol. **85** The Housing Crisis

Vol. **88** Food and Nutrition

Vol. **89** Refugees

Vol. **96** Preventing Sexual Diseases

Vol. **97** Energy Matters

Vol. **99** Exploited Children

Vol. **100** Stress and Anxiety

Vol. **103** Animal Rights

Vol. **106** Trends in Marriage

Vol. **107** Work Issues

Vol. **115** Racial Discrimination

Vol. **116** Grief and Loss

Vol. **117** Self-Esteem and Body Image

Vol. **118** Focus on Sport

Vol. **119** Transport Trends

Vol. **120** The Human Rights Issue

Vol. **121** The Censorship Debate

Vol. **122** Bullying

Vol. **123** Young People and Health

Vol. **124** Parenting Issues

Vol. **125** Understanding Depression

Vol. **126** The Abortion Debate

Vol. **127** Eating Disorders

Vol. **128** The Cannabis Issue

Vol. **129** Gambling Trends

Vol. **130** Homelessness

Vol. **131** Citizenship and National Identity

Vol. **132** Child Abuse

Vol. **133** Teen Pregnancy and Lone Parents

Vol. **134** Customers and Consumerism

Vol. **135** Coping with Disability

Vol. **136** Self-Harm

Vol. **137** Crime and Anti-Social Behaviour

Vol. **138** A Genetically Modified Future?

Vol. **139** The Education Problem

Vol. **140** Vegetarian and Vegan Diets

Vol. **141** Mental Health

Vol. **142** Media Issues

Vol. **143** Problem Drinking

Vol. **144** The Cloning Debate

Vol. **145** Smoking Trends

Vol. **146** Sustainability and Environment

Vol. **147** The Terrorism Problem

Vol. **148** Religious Beliefs

Vol. **149** A Classless Society?

Vol. **150** Migration and Population

Vol. **151** Climate Change

Vol. **152** Euthanasia and the Right to Die

Vol. **153** Sexual Orientation and Society

Vol. **154** The Gender Gap

Vol. **155** Domestic Abuse

Vol. **156** Travel and Tourism

Vol. **157** The Problem of Globalisation

Vol. **158** The Internet Revolution

Vol. **159** An Ageing Population

Vol. **160** Poverty and Exclusion

Vol. **161** Waste Issues

Vol. **162** Staying Fit

Vol. **163** Drugs in the UK

remote gambling **129**.17-26
remote sensing satellites and surveillance **120**.34
renewable energy **97**.6-18, 26; **151**.29-30
    advantages of **97**.9
    attitudes to **97**.5
    bioenergy **97**.5, 6, 9, 11, 18
    case for **97**.1-2, 6-7
    costs of **97**.19, 38
    defining **97**.8-9
    electricity from **97**.4, 11, 37-8
    future of **97**.8-9
    hydroelectric power **97**.4, 5, 6, 12, 14, 38
    and nuclear power **97**.6, 7, 19, 21
    sources of **97**.4
    types of **97**.9
    in the UK **97**.13-14, 26, 39
rent deposit schemes **130**.29
rented accommodation
    shortage **130**.8
    support services **130**.29
reprimands, and youth crime **137**.12
reproductive cloning **144**.15
reproductive rights, disabled people **135**.27
reproductive system, effects of eating disorders **127**.5
reprogrammed cells **144**.26
residential mobility **149**.26
resin, cannabis (hashish) **128**.1, 3, 6, 23
    seizures of **128**.31
resources
    natural **146**.9
    resource efficiency **146**.7
respiratory health
    and cannabis **128**.18-19
    lung cancer **128**.17, 19, 28; **145**.34
    and passive smoking **145**.29
responsibilities
    and children's rights **120**.1
    young people **120**.7-8
responsibility, encouraging children's **124**.13-14
responsible drinking **143**.26-7, 29
responsible travel **134**.30; **156**.1, 20-39
    definition **156**.24
restaurants
    and vegans **140**.25
    and vegetarians **140**.5
restorative justice **137**.12
restraint techniques in youth detention centres **120**.17
retail industry **107**.5
    and environmentalism **146**.38
    packaging waste **161**.12
    plastic bags **161**.13-14
retail therapy **134**.13
retirement
    age of **107**.13
    feelings about **159**.15
    and male depression **125**.15
    retiring abroad **150**.24
    saving for **159**.21, 22
    spending patterns, retired people **159**.19
    working after retirement age **159**.10, 15
reusing goods **161**.18

reverse anorexia **127**.19
RFID (Radio Frequency Identification) tags **82**.13-17, 35
    companies making or using **82**.13, 15-16, 35
    and crime **82**.17
    and data protection **82**.16
    defining **82**.13, 15
    disabling **82**.14
    identifying **82**.13-14
    media coverage of **82**.15
    possible consumer benefits of **82**.16-17
    and surveillance **82**.16
rhinoplasty, teenagers **117**.27
rice, GM contamination **138**.20, 31-4
rich-poor gap
    global **160**.26, 29
    UK **115**.32; **149**.19, 20, 22, 27, 29; **160**.6, 7
right-wing terrorism **147**.1
rights
    in abortion
        of the fetus **126**.21-2, 27
        of men **126**.15
        of women **126**.21
    children's *see* children's rights
    consumer *see* consumer rights
    of migrant workers **150**.2
    prisoners **137**.37-8
    to protest **121**.14
        about offensive material **121**.13
    young people **120**.1-22
    victims of crime **137**.28
rivers
    drying up of **76**.2, 35
    pollution **76**.4
        and freshwater supplies **76**.15
    and species extinction **78**.10
road accidents **119**.4, 5, 28, 30-31
    and children **119**.5, 28, 30-31
    deaths **119**.4, 5, 28, 30
    and speed **119**.5, 30-31
road building to ease congestion **119**.12
road charging **119**.35, 36
    congestion charging **119**.12, 34-5, 38
road safety **119**.4
    education **119**.5-6
    quiz **119**.6
road tax exemption, disabled people **135**.7
road traffic **119**.1
    carbon offsetting **151**.22
    increase **119**.11, 13, 29
    injuries, children **119**.5, 28, 30-31
    pollution *see* pollution and transport
role models
    boys **117**.23
    and self-esteem **117**.37
rough sleeping **130**.9-12
    Scotland **130**.6
round-the-world tickets **156**.15
RSPCA Freedom Food mark **140**.29, 34
rubbish *see* waste
running, effect on joints **162**.33
rural views and mental well-being **117**.38-9

S

sacred places **148**.1

SAD (Seasonal Affective Disorder) **125**.4, 18, 37-8; **141**.35

sadness, feelings after bereavement **116**.19

safe houses *see* refuges

safety
  of abortion **126**.14
  and alcohol **123**.17
    drinks labelling **143**.30, 31, 32
  and cycling **119**.28
  and gender equality **154**.3-4, 6
  of genetically modified crops **138**.6-6, 24
  of goods, consumer rights **134**.20
  and mobile phones **158**.13
  parents' fears **124**.13-14
  and social networking **158**.9, 10-11
  transport **119**.1
  and walking to school **119**.26
  at work **107**.31

safety and the Internet **132**.33
  children and young people **158**.27-30
  online shopping **158**.31

salaries
  graduates **139**.35, 36, 37
  teachers **139**.12

salmonella **88**.28

salt intake **88**.2, 7, 10, 16, 23, 26
  teenagers **123**.7

same-sex relationships and domestic abuse **155**.13-15

sanitation
  in developing countries **76**.7, 8, 12, 17, 21; **146**.14-15
  and the right to water **76**.24

saturated fats **88**.2, 22-3

savings
  attitudes to **74**.5
    children **74**.6-7
  for old age **159**.21, 22
  levels of **134**.25
  and parents **74**.7
  savings accounts

  for children **74**.13
    and young people **74**.19, 24
  and social class **149**.20
  and teenagers **74**.8-9
  and young people **74**.15

saying no **117**.3

scabies **96**.7

scalds, first aid **136**.23

scams **134**.26-9

schizophrenia **141**.4-5
  and cannabis use **128**.14-15

school bullying **122**.1-7; 11-12
  anti-bullying policies **122**.11, 18, 25
  and film violence **121**.28
  girls and young women **122**.10, 14, 15-16
  homophobic bullying **122**.3
  new school year **122**.12
  no-blame policy **122**.6-7
  peer support **122**.12
  racist bullying **122**.4-5

school holidays and bullying **122**.12

school leavers, lack of basic skills **139**.17

school leaving age **139**.1, 26

school meals
  children's attitudes to food in school **123**.32

schools
  absences, gender differences **154**.25
  academies **139**.14-16
  alcohol education in **143**.20
  behaviour problems **120**.16
  and children in developing countries **76**.13-14
  citizenship teaching **131**.36
  corporal punishment
    prohibion of **132**.15
    worldwide **132**.7
  costs **160**.16-17, 18, 19
  and drugs **163**.28-9
  and disabled children **135**.24-5
  and emergency planning **147**.31-2
  and ethnic minority children **115**.18, 19-21
  exclusions, gender differences **154**.24
  faith-based **148**.34, 35-6

Volume numbers appear first (in bold) followed by page numbers; a change in volume number is preceded by a semi-colon.

Vol. 74 Money Matters
Vol. 76 The Water Crisis
Vol. 78 Threatened Species
Vol. 81 Alternative Therapies
Vol. 82 Protecting our Privacy
Vol. 85 The Housing Crisis
Vol. 88 Food and Nutrition
Vol. 89 Refugees
Vol. 96 Preventing Sexual Diseases
Vol. 97 Energy Matters
Vol. 99 Exploited Children
Vol. 100 Stress and Anxiety
Vol. 103 Animal Rights
Vol. 106 Trends in Marriage
Vol. 107 Work Issues
Vol. 115 Racial Discrimination
Vol. 116 Grief and Loss
Vol. 117 Self-Esteem and Body Image
Vol. 118 Focus on Sport
Vol. 119 Transport Trends
Vol. 120 The Human Rights Issue
Vol. 121 The Censorship Debate

Vol. 122 Bullying
Vol. 123 Young People and Health
Vol. 124 Parenting Issues
Vol. 125 Understanding Depression
Vol. 126 The Abortion Debate
Vol. 127 Eating Disorders
Vol. 128 The Cannabis Issue
Vol. 129 Gambling Trends
Vol. 130 Homelessness
Vol. 131 Citizenship and National Identity
Vol. 132 Child Abuse
Vol. 133 Teen Pregnancy and Lone Parents
Vol. 134 Customers and Consumerism
Vol. 135 Coping with Disability
Vol. 136 Self-Harm
Vol. 137 Crime and Anti-Social Behaviour
Vol. 138 A Genetically Modified Future?
Vol. 139 The Education Problem
Vol. 140 Vegetarian and Vegan Diets
Vol. 141 Mental Health
Vol. 142 Media Issues
Vol. 143 Problem Drinking

Vol. 144 The Cloning Debate
Vol. 145 Smoking Trends
Vol. 146 Sustainability and Environment
Vol. 147 The Terrorism Problem
Vol. 148 Religious Beliefs
Vol. 149 A Classless Society?
Vol. 150 Migration and Population
Vol. 151 Climate Change
Vol. 152 Euthanasia and the Right to Die
Vol. 153 Sexual Orientation and Society
Vol. 154 The Gender Gap
Vol. 155 Domestic Abuse
Vol. 156 Travel and Tourism
Vol. 157 The Problem of Globalisation
Vol. 158 The Internet Revolution
Vol. 159 An Ageing Population
Vol. 160 Poverty and Exclusion
Vol. 161 Waste Issues
Vol. 162 Staying Fit
Vol. 163 Drugs in the UK

and global citizenship 131.37
and homophobia 153.14-18
intake, effect on attainment 149.31-3
and integration 115.29, 33
intelligent design, teaching 148.39
journeys to 119.25, 26-7, 29-30
and mental health education 141.37
multi-faith 148.32-3
nature studies 117.39
and physical activity 162.13
private, and university entrance 149.34-5
and physical activity 162.13
pupil-teacher ratio 139.12
and racism 115.9, 19-20
self-harm support 136.11, 18
sex education *see* sex education
sexual abuse education 132.27
single-sex 139.11-12
and special educational needs 135.36-9
sports 118.3, 4
statistics 139.1
teaching about money matters 74.1, 6, 12, 32-3
and university entrance 149.34-5
weighing children 127.36; 162.16
workforce, gender differences 154.25
young people and stress 100.1
young people's attitudes to 123.2-3
science education
   A-level choices 139.21-2
   gender differences 154.22-3
scientific research, and animal experiments 103.3
Scotland, Church of and ethics of human cloning 144.5-6
scratchcards and under 16s 129.12
screen violence, influence on children 121.28, 33, 34, 35
sea level rise 151.8; 157.2
seafood, sustainable 146.29
search engines 158.2, 25-6
Seasonal Affective Disorder (SAD) 125.4, 18, 37-8; 141.35
seasonal labour 89.22-3
second-hand goods, consumer rights 134.2
second-hand smoke *see* passive smoking
Second World War
   and family life 106.1
secondary schools
   curriculum 139.5-6
Secret Intelligence Service (MI6) 147.2
secure training centres, restraint techniques 120.17
security, national 147.2-3
security alerts 147.30
Security Service (MI5) 147.2
segregation 115.28-32
segregation indices 115.31-2
selective breeding 138.12
selenium
   in red meat 140.12
   and vegetarian diets 140.7
self-blame *see* blame, feelings of
self-censorship, broadcasters 121.36-7
self-criticism 117.6, 34
self-directed violence *see* self-harm; suicide
self-employment 107.2

self-esteem 117.1-9; 127.24
   contributory factors 117.4, 31-3
   definition 117.1, 31
   and eating disorders 127.2
   and green activities 117.38-9
   healthy 117.30
   high 117.5, 31
      and criminality 117.7
   improving 117.1-2, 6, 33-9; 136.3
      through learning and skills development 130.35
   low, and bullying 122.8
   questionnaire 117.9
self-harm 123.9, 36-9; 136.1-26
   age of self-harmers 136.4, 20
   asking for help 136.12-13, 21
   case studies 136.6, 15-16
   as coping strategy 136.10, 25
   definition 136.1, 4, 10, 17, 24
   and eating disorders 127.10
   as expression of feelings 136.10, 18
   in groups 136.8-9
   methods of 136.1, 7, 9, 17, 26
   minimizing damage 136.22-3
   myths about 136.8-9
   older people 136.20
   peer support 136.18
   prevalence 136.4, 7, 10
   prevention 136.4-5
   prisoners 137.37
   reasons for 123.37; 1-2, 4, 5, 7, 10, 17-18, 20
   risk factors 136.2, 10
   signs 136.9, 10-11
   sources of help 123.36-7; 136.3, 12-13, 21
   self-help 136.3, 19, 21
   stopping 136.3, 21
   and suicide 123.36; 136.2, 9, 11, 24-6
   treatment 136.11
   young people 136.2, 4-19
self-image *see* body image
self-injury 136.1-26
self-judgement 117.4
self-poisoning 136.26
self-reproach and traumatic bereavement 116.11
semantic web 158.25-6
sensory impairment and age 159.4
separation
   effect on children 124.33-4
   and male depression 125.14
   and the process of divorce 106.28
separation from parents, children's rights 120.11
separatism, Islam 147.18
serotonin 141.9
   and eating disorders 127.6-7
services and child labour 99.2, 4
sex, definition 154.1
sex discrimination 154.6
   in the workplace 154.30
   worldwide 154.13-14
sex education 123.20; 133.12-16
   age of children 133.15
   aims 133.13

and attitudes to sex **133**.14

and magazines **142**.28, 29

role of parents **133**.12, 15

about sexual abuse **132**.27

and underage sex **123**.21

sex offenders **132**.22, 25, 26

children as **132**.29, 30

help for **132**.36-9

travel restriction **156**.37

Sex and Relationships Education (SRE) **133**.12-13

sex stereotyping *see* gender stereotyping

sex tourism **156**.37-9

sex work and street lifestyle **130**.12

sexual abuse **132**.1, 22-39

and child domestic workers **99**.8, 9

effects **132**.4, 22, 23

getting help **132**.23-4, 28

and the Internet **132**.30, 31-2, 33

misunderstandings about **132**.25-6

of older people **159**.16-17

recovering from **132**.28

and self-harm **123**.37

and sex education **132**.27

signs of **132**.4

and stress **100**.1, 2

worldwide extent **132**.31

sexual abusers **132**.22

children as **132**.29, 30

help for **132**.36-9

sexual behaviour

and early sexual relationships **123**.21

and HIV **96**.12, 14, 16, 17

and male depression **125**.14

normal sexual behaviour of children **132**.29-30

and sexually transmitted infections **96**.9, 12

teenagers **123**.19-21; **133**.1-3

underage sex **123**.21

sexual exploitation of children **99**.1, 4, 16-18, 20-8

case studies **99**.21-2

harmful effects of **99**.16, 20

and poverty **99**.16, 24

and sex tourism **156**.37-9

teenagers **99**.20-2

and trafficking **99**.3, 16, 17, 18, 20, 21, 24, 28

sexual health and migrants **150**.21-3

sexual health clinics and STIs **123**.25

sexual identity confusion **149**.5

sexual imagery and TV watershed **121**.38

sexual intercourse

and the conception of children **123**.22

sexual orientation **153**.1-25

causes **153**.2, 6, 7

definition **153**.1

discovering **153**.1-2, 4, 7, 12

and the law **153**.26-39

modification therapy **153**.3

prejudice **153**.2-3

survey **153**.5

sexual relationships, changing attitudes to **106**.20

sexual rights, disabled people **135**.27

sexual violence **137**.8

sexualisation of young girls **154**.10

sexuality *see* sexual orientation

sexually transmitted infections (STIs) **96**.1-13; **123**.5, 24-6

avoiding **96**.1-2

bacterial **96**.3, 10, 12

chlamydia **96**.2-3, 4, 5, 8, 10, 12; **123**.26

genital herpes **96**.3, 4, 6, 10, 12

genital warts **96**.2-3, 4, 5-6, 12-13

gonorrhoea **96**.2, 3, 4, 5, 8, 10, 12

and HIV **96**.10, 12, 25

increase in **96**.4

pubic lice **96**.7

and sexual behaviour **96**.9, 12

symptoms of **96**.1, 5, 6, 7

syphilis **96**.3, 4, 6, 8, 10, 12

testing for **96**.1, 2, 3, 5, 6, 7, 10

treatment of **96**.1, 5, 6, 7, 10

trichomonas vaginalis **96**.6-7

types of **96**.2

in the UK **96**.2-3, 4

viral **96**.12-13

and young people **96**.3, 4, 8-9; **123**.3; **133**.2-3, 12-13, 17

sheep-goat chimera (geep) **144**.10

Volume numbers appear first (in bold) followed by page numbers; a change in volume number is preceded by a semi-colon.

Vol. **74** Money Matters

Vol. **76** The Water Crisis

Vol. **78** Threatened Species

Vol. **81** Alternative Therapies

Vol. **82** Protecting our Privacy

Vol. **85** The Housing Crisis

Vol. **88** Food and Nutrition

Vol. **89** Refugees

Vol. **96** Preventing Sexual Diseases

Vol. **97** Energy Matters

Vol. **99** Exploited Children

Vol. **100** Stress and Anxiety

Vol. **103** Animal Rights

Vol. **106** Trends in Marriage

Vol. **107** Work Issues

Vol. **115** Racial Discrimination

Vol. **116** Grief and Loss

Vol. **117** Self-Esteem and Body Image

Vol. **118** Focus on Sport

Vol. **119** Transport Trends

Vol. **120** The Human Rights Issue

Vol. **121** The Censorship Debate

Vol. **122** Bullying

Vol. **123** Young People and Health

Vol. **124** Parenting Issues

Vol. **125** Understanding Depression

Vol. **126** The Abortion Debate

Vol. **127** Eating Disorders

Vol. **128** The Cannabis Issue

Vol. **129** Gambling Trends

Vol. **130** Homelessness

Vol. **131** Citizenship and National Identity

Vol. **132** Child Abuse

Vol. **133** Teen Pregnancy and Lone Parents

Vol. **134** Customers and Consumerism

Vol. **135** Coping with Disability

Vol. **136** Self-Harm

Vol. **137** Crime and Anti-Social Behaviour

Vol. **138** A Genetically Modified Future?

Vol. **139** The Education Problem

Vol. **140** Vegetarian and Vegan Diets

Vol. **141** Mental Health

Vol. **142** Media Issues

Vol. **143** Problem Drinking

Vol. **144** The Cloning Debate

Vol. **145** Smoking Trends

Vol. **146** Sustainability and Environment

Vol. **147** The Terrorism Problem

Vol. **148** Religious Beliefs

Vol. **149** A Classless Society?

Vol. **150** Migration and Population

Vol. **151** Climate Change

Vol. **152** Euthanasia and the Right to Die

Vol. **153** Sexual Orientation and Society

Vol. **154** The Gender Gap

Vol. **155** Domestic Abuse

Vol. **156** Travel and Tourism

Vol. **157** The Problem of Globalisation

Vol. **158** The Internet Revolution

Vol. **159** An Ageing Population

Vol. **160** Poverty and Exclusion

Vol. **161** Waste Issues

Vol. **162** Staying Fit

Vol. **163** Drugs in the UK

sherry, strength of **143**.1
shock as response to bereavement **116**.3-4
shoes, recycling **161**.28
shopping
    addiction to **134**.13, 14
    and animal welfare **140**.31, 33
    and budgeting **74**.23
    and children **134**.12
    and energy efficiency **97**.31-2
    from home **82**.36-7
    Internet **134**.15-16; **158**.3, 30-31
    and money management **74**.17
    as social experience for women **134**.16
sibling trouble **124**.18
sickness absence **107**.6-8; **154**.18
Sikhism **148**.5
    and abortion and contraception **126**.2
    and faith schools **148**.35
    festivals **148**.5
    food rules **148**.5
    funerals **116**.34
simple carbohydrates **88**.2
singing, and building self-esteem **117**.33
single homelessness **130**.1-2
single parents *see* lone parents
single people
    and the cost of living **106**.13
    and the housing market **85**.7, 23-4
    living alone **85**.2
    men **106**.3, 12, 20
    women **106**.3, 20
single-sex education **139**.11-12; **154**.25, 26, 27
single-sex youth work **154**.5
sinsemilla (cannabis) **128**.1, 4
skills shortages **107**.31-3
skin, effects of smoking **145**.30
skunk (cannabis) **128**.2, 3-4, 13
    home growing **128**.3-4, 30-31
    mental health effects **128**.15
slander **142**.26
slavery **120**.29, 30-31
    and child labour **99**.1; **120**.18-19
sleep
    and exercise **141**.39
    and mental health **141**.34
    and stress **100**.19, 27, 29
sleep eating disorder (SED-NOS) **127**.18
sleeper effect, smoking **123**.13
sleeping rough *see* rough sleeping
slum tours **156**.33-5
smacking children **132**.8-21
    arguments against ban **132**.14
    children's feelings about **132**.19-21
    defence of **132**.9-11, 14
    and human rights **132**.9, 12-13, 16-17
    perpetrators **132**.20
    public opinion **132**.8, 18
'smarter justice' **137**.29-30
smoking
    age of smokers **145**.1
    anti-smoking advertising **145**.18-19

ban on smoking in public places *see* smoking ban
    cannabis **128**.8
        effects of **128**.5, 18-19
    children **123**.11-13; **145**.2-3
        attitudes to smoking **145**.20
        starting smoking **123**.11, 13
    costs of **145**.17, 38
        as deterrent **145**.3
    deaths from **145**.1, 4, 12, 22, 24; **163**.11
    giving up **145**.33, 35-9
        benefits **145**.27, 35
        numbers of people giving up **145**.1
        reasons for giving up **145**.15
    and health **145**.25-39
        benefits of giving up **145**.27, 35
        children **145**.2
        developing countries **145**.23
    and life expectancy **145**.21
    men **145**.21, 22
        and fertility **145**.32
    passive smoking **145**.2, 28-9
    sleeper effect **123**.13
    statistics **145**.1, 3, 4
    and stress **100**.19, 27, 31, 34, 35, 37
    withdrawal symptoms **145**.26-7
    women **145**.21, 22
        and fertility **145**.32
    workplace smoking ban **145**.14
    young people **123**.2, 8, 9, 11-13; **145**.3, 4
        influence of films on smoking habits **145**.9-10
        and the law **123**.12; **145**.3
        prevention **123**.12, 13
        reasons for smoking **145**.5
smoking ban (ban on smoking in public places) **145**.11-17
    effect on mental health staff **145**.39
    effect on mental health sufferers **145**.38-9
    effect on pubs **145**.13
    effect on tobacco industry **145**.16-17
    legal challenge **145**.15
    public attitudes **145**.13, 18
    and workplaces **145**.14
smuggling
    cigarettes **145**.17
    drugs **163**.37-8
soap bar (cannabis) **128**.1
soaps, TV
    and offensive language **121**.38
    and teenage drinking **143**.18-19
social care services
    and disabled people **135**.4
    expectations of **135**.18
    insuffiency **135**.20
    and older people **159**.4, 28, 26, 29
social class **149**.1-17
    and advertising **134**.8
    and attitudes to money **149**.19-20
    and attitudes to moving home **149**.26
    and children's nutrition **162**.13-14
    classification **149**.3, 5
    confusion over **149**.4
    and educational attainment **149**.30, 31-3; **154**.23

gender and pupil behaviour **154**.24-5
and mental health problems **141**.2
and obesity **162**.5
psychology of **149**.6
regional differences **149**.18
self-awareness of **149**.3, 4, 18, 19, 24
social and cultural globalisation **157**.2
social differences, children's perceptions of **149**.9-12
social exclusion
and education **160**.17-18
older people **159**.30
social factors and gambling **129**.7, 29
social gambling **129**.11, 18
social group classification system **149**.3, 5
social housing
government strategy **130**. 16, 33
shortage **130**. 8, 23
social identity theory and football support **141**.32-3
social inclusion effects of homelessness, children **130**. 23
social interaction and low self-esteem **117**.4
social isolation
older people **159**.3, 8, 17, 30
and self-harm **136**.18
social life and self-esteem **117**.36
social marketing and reducing consumption **161**.34
social mobility **160**.7
and education **139**.13; **149**.22, 25, 30, 36-7
international comparisons **149**.25
social model of disability **135**.1
social networking **142**.35, 36, 38; **158**.3, 9
and globalisation **157**.15
and mobile phones **158**.11-12
security **158**.9, 10-11
and travel **156**.14
social pressures
on athletes to use drugs **118**.29
and eating disorders **127**.2
social profiles by neighbourhood **149**.17, 23
social responsibility, corporate **157**.11
social roles and gender differences **154**.9
social security benefits *see* state benefits
social skills gap **149**.37-8

social status and ageing **159**.32
social therapies for depression **125**.26
social topography **149**.17, 23
social workers
and child protection **132**.3, 5
and stress in young people **100**.2
and workplace stress **100**.12
socio-economic deprivation, migrants **150**.22
socio-economic groups
and disability **135**.2
and news awareness **142**.31
and non-traditional families **124**.21
and obesity **162**.5
and smoking **145**.1, 21
sodium intake, teenagers **123**.7
soft segregation **115**.28
Soil Association standards
free-range eggs **140**.29, 39
organic farming **140**.35
soil management **88**.14
solar activity and global warming **151**.5-6
solar energy **97**.2, 4, 6, 8-9, 10, 21
costs of **97**.14
and energy efficiency **97**.31
market for **97**.14
PV (Photovoltaics) **97**.8, 9, 12, 13, 38
in the UK **97**.10, 13, 14, 26
soldiers, suicides, Japan **136**.39
solicitors for court hearings **137**.36
solid fuels, as a source of energy **97**.4
solvent abuse **163**.5-6
deaths from **163**.11
somatic-cell nuclear transfer (SCNT) **144**.1-2, 9, 26
soup runs **130**.31
souvenirs, wildlife **156**.32
soya products for vegetarians **140**.22, 23, 26
spa holidays 5
space
as a natural resource **146**.9
sustainable use of **146**.17
spam **82**.31-3, 36-7
Special Educational Needs (SEN) **135**.36-9

Volume numbers appear first (in bold) followed by page numbers; a change in volume number is preceded by a semi-colon.

Vol. **74** Money Matters
Vol. **76** The Water Crisis
Vol. **78** Threatened Species
Vol. **81** Alternative Therapies
Vol. **82** Protecting our Privacy
Vol. **85** The Housing Crisis
Vol. **88** Food and Nutrition
Vol. **89** Refugees
Vol. **96** Preventing Sexual Diseases
Vol. **97** Energy Matters
Vol. **99** Exploited Children
Vol. **100** Stress and Anxiety
Vol. **103** Animal Rights
Vol. **106** Trends in Marriage
Vol. **107** Work Issues
Vol. **115** Racial Discrimination
Vol. **116** Grief and Loss
Vol. **117** Self-Esteem and Body Image
Vol. **118** Focus on Sport
Vol. **119** Transport Trends
Vol. **120** The Human Rights Issue
Vol. **121** The Censorship Debate

Vol. **122** Bullying
Vol. **123** Young People and Health
Vol. **124** Parenting Issues
Vol. **125** Understanding Depression
Vol. **126** The Abortion Debate
Vol. **127** Eating Disorders
Vol. **128** The Cannabis Issue
Vol. **129** Gambling Trends
Vol. **130** Homelessness
Vol. **131** Citizenship and National Identity
Vol. **132** Child Abuse
Vol. **133** Teen Pregnancy and Lone Parents
Vol. **134** Customers and Consumerism
Vol. **135** Coping with Disability
Vol. **136** Self-Harm
Vol. **137** Crime and Anti-Social Behaviour
Vol. **138** A Genetically Modified Future?
Vol. **139** The Education Problem
Vol. **140** Vegetarian and Vegan Diets
Vol. **141** Mental Health
Vol. **142** Media Issues
Vol. **143** Problem Drinking

Vol. **144** The Cloning Debate
Vol. **145** Smoking Trends
Vol. **146** Sustainability and Environment
Vol. **147** The Terrorism Problem
Vol. **148** Religious Beliefs
Vol. **149** A Classless Society?
Vol. **150** Migration and Population
Vol. **151** Climate Change
Vol. **152** Euthanasia and the Right to Die
Vol. **153** Sexual Orientation and Society
Vol. **154** The Gender Gap
Vol. **155** Domestic Abuse
Vol. **156** Travel and Tourism
Vol. **157** The Problem of Globalisation
Vol. **158** The Internet Revolution
Vol. **159** An Ageing Population
Vol. **160** Poverty and Exclusion
Vol. **161** Waste Issues
Vol. **162** Staying Fit
Vol. **163** Drugs in the UK

gender differences 154.24

and mainstream schooling 135.37-9

special schools 135.36

specialist diplomas 139.23-5

species boundaries 144.12

spectacles, recycling 161.28

spectators, pressure on athletes to use drugs 118.23

speed cameras 119.4, 17, 18

speed limiters 119.18

speed limits

and active traffic management 119.37-8

raising 119.4

speeding 119.3, 4, 8

and pedestrian injuries 119.5, 30-31

spending 134.3-4

on advertising 134.7

on credit cards 134.24

on education 139.1

on ethical products 134.31, 32

older people 159.19

on tourism 156.5, 10

sperm cell creation from bone marrow 144.29

spermicides 123.23

spin, government 121.17-18

spin doctors 131.18

spinal damage, stem cell therapy 144.21

spirits

strength of 143.1

young people's drinking 123.1

spirituality 148.1

interest in 148.19

spoiled children as bullies 122.9-10

sponsorship and women's sport 118.21

sport

benefits for young people 137.29

betting 129.2

and drugs 118.23-39

and inclusion 118.12-22

participation see participation in sport

trends 118.1-11

sports facilities 118.5-6

spot-reduction of fat 162.33

spread betting 129.2

spyware 158.34

and domestic abuse 155.15-16

SSRIs (Selective Serotonin Re-Uptake Inhibitors) 123.28; 125.8, 10, 32

Staphylococcus aureus 88.29

starchy foods 88.5-6, 12

state benefits 160.23-4

for asylum seekers 89.12, 13, 14, 19, 30, 38

benefit problems

and debt 130.25

and homelessness 130.9, 12

after bereavement 116.30

Child Tax Credit 74.7; 133.33

costs of incapacity benefit 100.23

Council Tax Benefit, lone parents 133.35, 38

disabled people 135.3, 4, 5-6

low take-up 135.18

Housing Benefit 133.34-5

problems, and homelessness 130.9

jobseekers' allowance 100.23

and lone parents 133.33-6, 37, 38

amount discrepancies 133.36

encouraging single parenthood 133.32

and migrants 150.7

and students 74.39

Working Families Tax Credit 74.7

Working Tax Credit 133.35

state pension 159.3, 23

state religion 148.21-2

state-sanctioned violence on children 120.17

statutory homelessness 130.2-3, 13

steel cans recycling 161.27

stem cell lines 144.18

personalized 144.25

stem cell research 144.2, 15-29

ethical issues 144.6, 17

how it works 144.16

public attitudes to 138.16; 144.19

timeline 144.27-8, 33

using hybrid embryos 144.14

stem cell therapy 144.17-18, 21-6, 28

stem cells 144.15, 17-18

from bone marrow 144.21, 23

stepfamilies 124.23-8, 39

benefits 124.25

children's worries 124.23, 26

parents' worries 124.27-8

statistics 106.3-4; 124.23, 24, 25

step-parenting 124.39

sterile-seed (Terminator) technology 138.18

steroids see anabolic agents/steroids

stimulants (uppers) 118.36-7; 163.2, 4-5

stop and search rights 128.35; 147.35-7

stopping cannabis use 128.2, 10

stopping smoking see smoking, giving up

store cards 134.22

storms, and climate change 151.8

stratosphere cooling 151.4

street children 99.1, 18-19

as tourist sights 156.33-4

street drinking 130.12

street homelessness 130.9-12

numbers 130.9-10

reasons for 130.10-11

street lifestyles 130.12

stress 107.8, 18

avoiding 141.36

and anxiety 100.2, 21

coping with 100.27-39

defining 100.1, 5, 33

and eating disorders 127.16

and exercise 141.39; 162.37

factors determining degree of 100.14-15

'fight or flight' response to 100.1, 14-15, 25, 28

harmful effects of 100.28, 38

health benefits of the right sort of 100.39

and lifestyle 100.19, 31-2

positive and negative 100.14

reduction and self-esteem 117.33

signs and symptoms of **100**.1, 2, 5, 12, 28-9, 33, 35
   statistics on **100**.13, 19
   and workplace bullying **122**.30, 37
stress management **100**.32, 36
strokes **159**.4
   and depression **125**.5
   stem cell therapy **144**.22
structural adjustment **157**.7
students **107**.33, 35-6
   applying to university **139**.29-32
     and parental educational level **149**.7, 31, 35
   health issues **123**.4-5
   living at home **149**.2
   and money matters **74**.1, 17, 19-22, 28-32, 34-9; **134**.24; **139**.34-5
     bank accounts **74**.1, 2, 17, 21-2, 29, 32
     budgeting **74**.2, 28, 30, 32
     bursaries **74**.32, 37
     costs of a university education **74**.38; **139**.34, 35
     course costs **74**.30
     credit cards **74**.3, 30, 32, 36, 37
     debts **74**.1, 3, 5, 19-20, 28-9, 31-2, 34-9
     disabled students **74**.39
     estimated average student expenditure **74**.29
     graduate starting salaries **74**.31; **139**.35, 36
     grants **74**.39
     hardship funds **74**.37
     living and study costs **74**.28, 30
     loans **139**.34
     overdrafts **74**.1, 21-2, 37
     and paid employment **74**.20, 29, 37
     part-time work **139**.35
     and parents **74**.19, 38
     and state benefits **74**.39
     tuition fees **74**.19, 20, 31, 37, 39
     university access funds **74**.39
   opinions on abortion for disability **126**.35
   from overseas, entry allowed **150**.23
   statistics **139**.2, 32
   and terrorism **147**.13-14
substance abuse
   and homelessness **130**.11, 20

young people **123**.17
success, attitude to, and self-esteem **117**.8
suction termination (abortion) **126**.14
suicidal feelings
   after bereavement **116**.4
   children **123**.35
suicide **136**.27-39
   bereavement by **116**.8
   and depression **125**.10, 22
   impact on others **136**.28
   and the Internet **136**.37-9
   and the media **136**.37; **142**.30
   men **125**.15
   prevention
     how to help **136**.29
     initiatives **136**.31, 32, 36
   prisoners **137**.37
   reasons for **136**.27
   risk factors for **136**.25-6, 27, 30
   and self-harm **136**.2, 9, 11, 24-6
   statistics **125**.16; **136**.31, 33, 34, 35; **137**.8
   suicide pacts and the Internet **136**.39
   support for suicidal people **136**.27-8
     Samaritans **136**.29, 32, 37
   warning signs of **136**.11, 29, 30
sulphur dioxide (SO2) emissions **119**.15; **146**.35
supercasinos **129**.14-16, 34
supermarkets
   and Fairtrade **134**.36
   and free-range eggs **140**.38
   and GM products **138**.26
   impact on communities **134**.38
   packaging waste **161**.12
   and plastic bags **161**.13-14
   and vegetarianism **140**.20
supplements **118**.35
   and anti-doping rules **118**.33
   nutritional **118**.28
support groups
   abortion **126**.7
   alcohol abuse **143**.38, 39
   domestic abuse perpetrators **155**.33-4

Volume numbers appear first (in bold) followed by page numbers; a change in volume number is preceded by a semi-colon.

Vol. **74** Money Matters
Vol. **76** The Water Crisis
Vol. **78** Threatened Species
Vol. **81** Alternative Therapies
Vol. **82** Protecting our Privacy
Vol. **85** The Housing Crisis
Vol. **88** Food and Nutrition
Vol. **89** Refugees
Vol. **96** Preventing Sexual Diseases
Vol. **97** Energy Matters
Vol. **99** Exploited Children
Vol. **100** Stress and Anxiety
Vol. **103** Animal Rights
Vol. **106** Trends in Marriage
Vol. **107** Work Issues
Vol. **115** Racial Discrimination
Vol. **116** Grief and Loss
Vol. **117** Self-Esteem and Body Image
Vol. **118** Focus on Sport
Vol. **119** Transport Trends
Vol. **120** The Human Rights Issue
Vol. **121** The Censorship Debate

Vol. **122** Bullying
Vol. **123** Young People and Health
Vol. **124** Parenting Issues
Vol. **125** Understanding Depression
Vol. **126** The Abortion Debate
Vol. **127** Eating Disorders
Vol. **128** The Cannabis Issue
Vol. **129** Gambling Trends
Vol. **130** Homelessness
Vol. **131** Citizenship and National Identity
Vol. **132** Child Abuse
Vol. **133** Teen Pregnancy and Lone Parents
Vol. **134** Customers and Consumerism
Vol. **135** Coping with Disability
Vol. **136** Self-Harm
Vol. **137** Crime and Anti-Social Behaviour
Vol. **138** A Genetically Modified Future?
Vol. **139** The Education Problem
Vol. **140** Vegetarian and Vegan Diets
Vol. **141** Mental Health
Vol. **142** Media Issues
Vol. **143** Problem Drinking

Vol. **144** The Cloning Debate
Vol. **145** Smoking Trends
Vol. **146** Sustainability and Environment
Vol. **147** The Terrorism Problem
Vol. **148** Religious Beliefs
Vol. **149** A Classless Society?
Vol. **150** Migration and Population
Vol. **151** Climate Change
Vol. **152** Euthanasia and the Right to Die
Vol. **153** Sexual Orientation and Society
Vol. **154** The Gender Gap
Vol. **155** Domestic Abuse
Vol. **156** Travel and Tourism
Vol. **157** The Problem of Globalisation
Vol. **158** The Internet Revolution
Vol. **159** An Ageing Population
Vol. **160** Poverty and Exclusion
Vol. **161** Waste Issues
Vol. **162** Staying Fit
Vol. **163** Drugs in the UK

domestic abuse sufferers 155.6-7, 28-9
gamblers 129.37
self-harmers 136.3, 21
sexual abusers 132.37-9
surgery
and animal research 103.3
weight loss 162.3
surgical dilation and evacuation (abortion) 126.10, 14
surname choice of women 154.19-20
surrogacy and parents' rights 153.34
surveillance 82.17-19; 120.33-4; 147.29
and facial recognition technology 82.3
and the Government 82.1-3, 22, 23
mass surveillance technologies 82.1
and RFID tags 82.16
workplace 120.32-3
sustainability 146.1-11
construction industry 146.11
consumption 146.7, 8
definition 146.3
fossil fuels 151.28-30
Millennium Development Goals 160.32
production 146.7, 8
seafood 146.29
UK principles 146.3
UK strategy 146.8-9
sustainable agriculture 88.32-3; 146.27
sustainable communities 146.9
sustainable development
and global water supplies 76.17, 31
sustainable housing 85.1, 9
in rural areas 85.5
and sustainable communities 85.32, 38, 39
sustainable population 150.31-2
sustainable tourism 156.8, 22-3, 24
attitudes to 156.29-30
sustainable use of space 146.17
swearing on television 121.38-9
sweatshops 157.27-9
sweepstake scams 134.26

T

t-GURTS 138.18
tabloid newspapers 142.8
tagging of asylum seekers 89.36-7
tai chi 81.3, 14, 30, 31, 39
talking therapies 125.29-30; 141.35
access to 125.30-31
tariffs see trade barriers
taxation
on aviation fuel 119.16
carbon tax on fuel 97.25
Child Tax Credit (CTC) 133.33
overpayments to lone-parent families 124.35; 133.30
and civil partnerships 153.28
congestion tax 119.34
contributions 89.23, 30
fraud and error 133.36
fuel taxes 119.14, 24

gambling 129.18
and income inequality 160.6
landfill tax 161.12, 20, 35
tobacco 145.17
and trade 157.12-13
Working Tax Credit 133.35
taxis and disabled people 135.9
tea, fairtrade 157.33-4
teachers
awareness of mobile bullying 122.25
gender gap 154.25
homophobic bullying 153.14, 16, 17
numbers of 139.1, 12
salaries 139.12
and stress in young people 100.1
and workplace stress 100.12
technology and bullying 122.5, 19-26
teenage fathers 133.25-7
teenage magazines 142.28
teenage mothers 133.18-24
education 133.24
public attitudes to 133.18, 21
single mothers 133.28
teenage parenthood, long-term effects 133.10
teenage parents 133.20-27
teenage pregnancies 126.30-31
and abortion 126.29; 133.9
under 16s and confidentiality 126.13, 28, 29
and adoption 133.8-9
advice 133.8
as biologically natural 133.19
keeping the baby 133.8
options 133.8-9
planned 133.20
and poverty 133.20
and single parents 126.31
statistics 126.30-31; 133.2, 4, 5-6, 12, 17
teenagers see young people
telecommunications, broadband 158.5-6
telephones
competitions 158.6
government surveillance of 82.1, 22, 23
mobile see mobile phones
telephone sales and consumer rights 134.20
workplace monitoring of calls 82.27
television 158.5
advertising and children 134.10, 12
alcohol advertising 143.19, 20
and body image 117.11-12
children 117.22
children's viewing 121.27
control of 158.32
and disabled people 135.29, 32, 35
and homosexuality 153.23-5
influence on young people 145.6
as news source 142.33
offensive language 121.38-9
online 158.21-2
reality television, promoting racial understanding 115.22
regulation 121.36-7
soaps

and offensive language 121.38

and teenage drinking 143.18-19

watershed 121.37, 38-9

and women's sport 118.21

young people's viewing habits 142.38

teleworking *see* homeworking

telomeres and ageing 159.32, 33; 162.12

temperature of the earth

'hockey stick' graph 151.15

measurement errors 151.4-5

temporary accommodation 130.9

numbers of households 130.5, 13-14

and older people 130.18

tenancy support services 130.29

terminally ill people

assisted suicide *see* assisted suicide

euthanasia *see* euthanasia

termination *see* abortion

Terminator (sterile-seed) technology 138.18

terms of trade 157.7

terrorism 147.1-25

and aviation security 82.3

countering 147.26-39

definition 147.1, 4

deportation of suspects 120.38-9

fear of 147.12

history 147.1, 4-5

and identity cards 82.2, 9, 10, 11; 120.35; 131.14

and the Internet 147.8-9

and Islamophobia 131.11

London bombings 115.27, 36

reaction to 147.10-11, 38-9

statistics 147.6

targeting terrorist funds 147.3, 28-9

Terrorism Acts 147.3, 27, 35-6

timeline 147.5

effect on tourism 156.8

types 147.1

tetrahydrocannabinol *see* THC

text messages

bullying 122.5, 19, 21, 22-3, 24, 25

preventing unwanted texts 134.28

textile industry, working conditions 157.27-9

textiles recycling 161.25, 28

THC (delta-9 tetrahydrocannabinol)

and cannabis strength 128.3

effect on brain 128.34

therapeutic cloning 144.2, 15, 16, 26

embryonic stem cells 144.25

humanist view of 144.7

therapeutic exemption forms 118.31-2

Third World 157.7

threatened environments as tourist destinations 156.27

tidal energy 97.2, 6, 12

timber production 146.30-31

timber recycling 161.25

time limit for abortion 126.12, 36-8

time management, and stress 100.27, 29, 32, 36

tiredness and bereavement 116.19

tissue cultures 103.17, 19, 22

TNCs *see* transnational corporations

tobacco

advertising ban 145.7

chemical contents of smoke 145.1

consumption 145.4, 22

deaths 163.11

and the economy 145.22-3

and pharming of HIV drugs 138.21-2

plants 145.25

production 145.22-3

tobacco industry

control of 145.23, 24

effect of smoking ban 145.16-17

toilets, lack of in developing countries 146.14-15

tolerance

to alcohol 143.7

to drugs 163.2

tomatoes, genetically modified 138.14

TOMPS (toxic organic micropollutants) 146.35-6

tools, recycling 161.25

torture

evidence obtained under torture 120.39

victims 89.18-20

touch screen software 158.22-3

Volume numbers appear first (in bold) followed by page numbers; a change in volume number is preceded by a semi-colon.

Vol. **74** Money Matters

Vol. **76** The Water Crisis

Vol. **78** Threatened Species

Vol. **81** Alternative Therapies

Vol. **82** Protecting our Privacy

Vol. **85** The Housing Crisis

Vol. **88** Food and Nutrition

Vol. **89** Refugees

Vol. **96** Preventing Sexual Diseases

Vol. **97** Energy Matters

Vol. **99** Exploited Children

Vol. **100** Stress and Anxiety

Vol. **103** Animal Rights

Vol. **106** Trends in Marriage

Vol. **107** Work Issues

Vol. **115** Racial Discrimination

Vol. **116** Grief and Loss

Vol. **117** Self-Esteem and Body Image

Vol. **118** Focus on Sport

Vol. **119** Transport Trends

Vol. **120** The Human Rights Issue

Vol. **121** The Censorship Debate

Vol. **122** Bullying

Vol. **123** Young People and Health

Vol. **124** Parenting Issues

Vol. **125** Understanding Depression

Vol. **126** The Abortion Debate

Vol. **127** Eating Disorders

Vol. **128** The Cannabis Issue

Vol. **129** Gambling Trends

Vol. **130** Homelessness

Vol. **131** Citizenship and National Identity

Vol. **132** Child Abuse

Vol. **133** Teen Pregnancy and Lone Parents

Vol. **134** Customers and Consumerism

Vol. **135** Coping with Disability

Vol. **136** Self-Harm

Vol. **137** Crime and Anti-Social Behaviour

Vol. **138** A Genetically Modified Future?

Vol. **139** The Education Problem

Vol. **140** Vegetarian and Vegan Diets

Vol. **141** Mental Health

Vol. **142** Media Issues

Vol. **143** Problem Drinking

Vol. **144** The Cloning Debate

Vol. **145** Smoking Trends

Vol. **146** Sustainability and Environment

Vol. **147** The Terrorism Problem

Vol. **148** Religious Beliefs

Vol. **149** A Classless Society?

Vol. **150** Migration and Population

Vol. **151** Climate Change

Vol. **152** Euthanasia and the Right to Die

Vol. **153** Sexual Orientation and Society

Vol. **154** The Gender Gap

Vol. **155** Domestic Abuse

Vol. **156** Travel and Tourism

Vol. **157** The Problem of Globalisation

Vol. **158** The Internet Revolution

Vol. **159** An Ageing Population

Vol. **160** Poverty and Exclusion

Vol. **161** Waste Issues

Vol. **162** Staying Fit

Vol. **163** Drugs in the UK

tour operators **156**.1, 8-9
tourism
    best and worst sights **156**.6
    child sex tourism **99**.17, 20, 23, 25-6; **156**.37-9
    and climate change **156**.1, 25, 28-30
    dependency on **156**.21
    effects of **156**.20-39
    environmental impact **156**.20, 21, 22, 25
    gap years **156**.15-19
    industry **156**.8-9
    Internet bookings **156**.1, 13, 14
    statistics **156**.3-4, 7, 10
    trends **156**.1-14
    visits to the UK **156**.3-4, 10, 13
tourists
    behaviour **156**.31
    unconcerned about environmental impact **156**.28-30
    visiting threatened environments **156**.27
tower blocks and racial segregation **115**.32
toxic chemicals
    and water pollution **76**.11
toxic organic micropollutants (TOMPS) **146**.35-6
trade, international see international trade
trade in endangered species **78**.16-17, 19-22; **146**.34
    and traditional medicine **78**.23
    and the UK **78**.38-9
trade liberalisation **157**.12, 20
trade rules **157**.17
    fairness **157**.17-18, 25
trade unions **107**.31
    and workplace stress **100**.11, 26
trading standards **88**.38-9
traffic see road traffic
traffic pollution see pollution and transport
trafficking **120**.28, 29
    and child labour **99**.1, 3, 4; **120**.18
    and the sexual exploitation of children **99**.3, 16, 17, 20,
        21, 24, 28
    women **150**.15
training
    and age discrimination **159**.9
    disabled people **135**.15
    opportunities, racial discrimination **115**.14
    and starting a business **107**.4, 34
    and workplace stress **100**.16
trains see railways
transgender people **153**.13
    and equality **154**.4
transgenic bacteria **144**.11
transnational corporations (TNCs) **157**.7
    and the environment **157**.10-11
transport
    census information **150**.36
    and climate change reduction **151**.39
    and disabled people **135**.7-9
    emissions see emissions, transport
    and energy efficiency **97**.24, 25, 31
    environmental **134**.30, 32
    public attitudes to **97**.35, 36
    spending on **134**.4, 25
    trends **119**.1-16, 29-31; **161**.31-2

transsexualism **149**.5; **153**.13
transvestism **153**.13
trauma memory **137**.9
traumatic bereavements **116**.10-12
travel
    documents **89**.33, 35
    ethical **134**.30
    and terrorism **147**.32
travel 2.0 sites **156**.14
travel agents **156**.9
treatment
    acne **123**.28
    alcohol abuse **143**.35, 38-9
    chlamydia **123**.26
    depression **123**.28; **125**.24-39
    eating disorders **123**.34; **127**.28-9
        binge eating **127**.16
        bulimia **127**.14
    manic depression **125**.19-20
    obesity **127**.34; **162**.2-3, 6, 20
    post-natal depression **125**.17-18
    Seasonal Affective Disorder **125**.18
    self-harm **136**.11
treats and self-esteem **117**.37
trees
    planting and carbon offsetting **151**.35
    planting as way of remembrance **116**.17
tricyclics **125**.32
troposphere warming **151**.4
truancy rates **139**.2
TVP (textured vegetable protein) **140**.19
two-earner families **149**.28

U

U film classification **121**.29
UK
    armed forces recruitment age **120**.20
    and children's rights **120**.2
    domestic tourisn **156**.10
    drugs policy criticized **128**.38
    ecological debt **146**.4-6
    economy
        benefits from globalisation **157**.1
        competition from overseas **157**.35-6
    genetically modified crops **138**.2-3, 5, 39
    Human Rights Act **120**.25-7
    identity cards **120**.35-6
    income inequality **160**.6, 7
    natural environment conservation **146**.32-3
    online gambling market **129**.19, 20
    population, ethnic groups **115**.3
    poverty **160**.1-24
    and refugee children **120**.21
    and sustainable development **146**.3, 8-9
    supercasino **129**.14-16
    tourism industry **156**.7-10, 13
    tourist sights **156**.6
    travel abroad **156**.1, 4
UN see United Nations

underachievement, black pupils 115.19-21
underage drinking 137.14
   and depression 125.9
   ideas for reducing 143.5, 29
   underage purchase of alcohol 143.16, 20, 28
underage gambling 129.1
   National Lottery 129.11-13
   online gambling 129.18, 25
   online poker 129.25
   Scotland 129.32-3
underage purchase of tobacco 145.3
underage sex 123.21
   abortion and confidentiality 126.13, 28, 29
undergraduates see students
underground travel and disabled people 135.9
unemployment 107.10, 37-9
   and depression, men 125.14-15
   disabled people 135.3
   housing and environmental decline 85.14
   and incapacity benefit 100.23
   jobseekers allowance (JSA) 100.23
   and migration 150.9-10
   and poverty 160.2
   young people 149.38-9
union jack 131.3-4
unions 107.31
unipolar (endogenous) depression 125.4, 10
uniqueness, and self-esteem 117.1
United Nations (UN) 157.8
   and school bullying policy 122.11
   and child labour 120.20
   and right to participation 120.9-10
   and right to vote 120.7
units of alcohol 123.16; 143.1, 26
   awareness of 143.11
   drink labelling 143.30, 32
Universal classification, films 121.29
universal social pension 159.24
universities
   admissions and exam stress 100.7
   and animal rights activists 103.15
   application numbers 139.31, 32

costs of a university education 74.38; 139.34, 35
courses 139.2, 29, 30, 38-9
discrimination against middle-class applications 149.7
'dumbing down' accusations 149.7
fees 139.34
funding 74.19-20
and integration 115.30
post-qualification admission 139.16
school background of students 149.34-5
selection and parental education 149.7, 31, 35
and social class 149.1-2
unmarried parents 124.22
upbringing and gender development 154.1
uppers see stimulants
urban areas and climate change 151.10-12
urban growth 146.17, 24
urbanization 150.33, 35, 37-8
utilitarian drug use 163.1

V

v-GURTs 138.18
vaccination
   and organic farming 140.35-6
vaccine damage compensation 135.5
vacuum aspiration (abortion) 126.14
value for money, and consumer rights 134.2
values
   and Britishness 131.1
   human 148.15
   religious 148.16
vascular dementia 141.6
vascular diseases and depression 125.5
veganism 140.2, 7, 25-6
   costs of 140.25
   and health 140.25
   and protein 140.23-4
   and restaurants 140.25
vegetables see fruit and vegetables
vegetarian diets 140.2, 6, 7
vegetarianism 88.18; 140.1-26

Volume numbers appear first (in bold) followed by page numbers; a change in volume number is preceded by a semi-colon.

Vol. **74** Money Matters
Vol. **76** The Water Crisis
Vol. **78** Threatened Species
Vol. **81** Alternative Therapies
Vol. **82** Protecting our Privacy
Vol. **85** The Housing Crisis
Vol. **88** Food and Nutrition
Vol. **89** Refugees
Vol. **96** Preventing Sexual Diseases
Vol. **97** Energy Matters
Vol. **99** Exploited Children
Vol. **100** Stress and Anxiety
Vol. **103** Animal Rights
Vol. **106** Trends in Marriage
Vol. **107** Work Issues
Vol. **115** Racial Discrimination
Vol. **116** Grief and Loss
Vol. **117** Self-Esteem and Body Image
Vol. **118** Focus on Sport
Vol. **119** Transport Trends
Vol. **120** The Human Rights Issue
Vol. **121** The Censorship Debate

Vol. **122** Bullying
Vol. **123** Young People and Health
Vol. **124** Parenting Issues
Vol. **125** Understanding Depression
Vol. **126** The Abortion Debate
Vol. **127** Eating Disorders
Vol. **128** The Cannabis Issue
Vol. **129** Gambling Trends
Vol. **130** Homelessness
Vol. **131** Citizenship and National Identity
Vol. **132** Child Abuse
Vol. **133** Teen Pregnancy and Lone Parents
Vol. **134** Customers and Consumerism
Vol. **135** Coping with Disability
Vol. **136** Self-Harm
Vol. **137** Crime and Anti-Social Behaviour
Vol. **138** A Genetically Modified Future?
Vol. **139** The Education Problem
Vol. **140** Vegetarian and Vegan Diets
Vol. **141** Mental Health
Vol. **142** Media Issues
Vol. **143** Problem Drinking

Vol. **144** The Cloning Debate
Vol. **145** Smoking Trends
Vol. **146** Sustainability and Environment
Vol. **147** The Terrorism Problem
Vol. **148** Religious Beliefs
Vol. **149** A Classless Society?
Vol. **150** Migration and Population
Vol. **151** Climate Change
Vol. **152** Euthanasia and the Right to Die
Vol. **153** Sexual Orientation and Society
Vol. **154** The Gender Gap
Vol. **155** Domestic Abuse
Vol. **156** Travel and Tourism
Vol. **157** The Problem of Globalisation
Vol. **158** The Internet Revolution
Vol. **159** An Ageing Population
Vol. **160** Poverty and Exclusion
Vol. **161** Waste Issues
Vol. **162** Staying Fit
Vol. **163** Drugs in the UK

definition **140**.1, 5
eating out **140**.5, 25
and food ingredients **140**.18
number of vegetarians **140**.20, 39
reasons for becoming vegetarian **140**.1, 5, 8, 14
and supermarkets **140**.20
vehicles
adaptations for diability **135**.7
recycling **161**.23
venison consumption **140**.15
veterinary research **103**.10
vicarious liability for racism at work **115**.12
victimization **153**.38
and racism **115**.7-8
at work **115**.11-12
victims of abuse
blamed for abuse **155**.2, 3
male **155**.12-13
misunderstandings about **132**.25-6
reasons for not leaving **155**.5, 6, 7
reluctance to speak out **155**.3-4, 30-31
support for **155**.6-7, 28-9
treatment for **132**.5, 24, 28
victims of crime **137**.4, 9-10, 29
likelihood of becoming an offender **137**.14
racial identity **115**.10
and release of offenders **137**.28
rights **137**.28
victim personal statement **137**.31
young people as **137**.13, 17
video games
and children **121**.32-3
video sharing sites **142**.35
videos
and children **121**.26
onine **158**.21-2
regulation **121**.26, 31
violence
against girls **154**.13-14
children as victims of **120**.17
and computer games **121**.33, 35; **158**.33
effect of corporal punishment **132**.10
disabled people as victims **135**.27
and male depression **125**.15
in the media **121**.34
effect on children **121**.28, 33, 34, 35
physical restraint in youth detention centres **120**.17
violent crime
effects on victims **137**.9-10
statistics **137**.7-8
violent extremism **147**.33-4
viruses, GM, to kill insects **138**.13-14
vitamins **140**.4
in meat **140**.12
Vocational Certificate of Education (VCE) **139**.18
vocational degree subjects **139**.38-9
vocational qualifications **139**.4, 18
gender difference **139**.10
vocational training and age discrimination **159**.9
volatile organic compounds **146**.35
volatile substance abuse *see* solvent abuse

voluntary activity, England **131**.3
gap years **156**.15-19
voluntary classification, video games **121**.33
voluntary euthanasia *see* assisted suicide
voting **131**.16, 17, 18
eligibility to vote **131**.16, 18, 30
lowering voting age **120**.7-8; **131**.28, 29, 30
reasons for not voting **131**.22
voter apathy **131**.22
voter turnout **131**.19-21

W

wages
and child domestic workers **99**.9, 10
footballers **118**.11
effect of immigration **150**.17
migrant workers **150**.9
minimum wage **107**.31
multinational companies **157**.11
for students **74**.37
waist measurement and exercise **162**.36
walking
as alternative to car **119**.25
health benefits of **119**.27
to school **119**.25, 26, 27
walking bus **119**.6, 26
war
effect on disabled people **135**.26
on terror **89**.8
war-affected children **99**.32-5
and the effects of armed conflict **99**.33
help for **99**.34
problem of **99**.32
testimonials of **99**.33-4
warranties, consumer rights **134**.18-19
waste
amounts **161**.1, 3-5, 22
as animal food **140**.17
collection **161**.6
construction industry **146**.11
definition **161**.1
and energy generation **97**.37, 39; **161**.20, 38, 39
food **161**.4, 10-11, 19
government strategy **161**.20
hazardous **161**.1, 6, 32
incineration **161**.7
reducing waste **161**.18, 19, 20, 38
sorting **161**.25
and water consumption **76**.1, 4, 19, 32, 36
waste hierarchy **161**.7, 18
water abstraction, and wildlife **76**.34
water companies **88**.31
contact with schools **76**.1
multinational water corporations **76**.22, 23, 29-30
responsibilities of **76**.1
and water bills in the UK **76**.33
and water conservation **76**.36
water conservation **76**.1, 3, 22, 37-9
answering questions about **76**.36

in everyday life **76**.27
in the garden **76**.1, 36, 37, 38
in the home **76**.37, 38
investment in **76**.27
in schools **76**.39
and showers **76**.1, 27, 37, 38
and toilet flushing **76**.2, 27, 37, 38
water consumption
bottled water **76**.23, 27
clean water as measure of poverty **160**.28
and eco-systems **76**.2, 16-17, 19
groundwater sources for drinking **76**.7, 9, 12
and the importance of water quality **76**.9
lack of access to clean water **76**.8, 9
largest users of water **76**.36
per capita household water consumption by region **76**.26
and population growth **76**.22, 29
reasons for growth in **76**.3, 5, 8
in selected countries **76**.7
statistics **76**.7, 9
and waste **76**.1, 4, 19, 32, 36
water requirements per person per day **76**.6
and water shortages **76**.21-2
water cycle **76**.2, 21
water filters, recycling **161**.25
water management
and agriculture **76**.18
costs of **76**.33
dealing with the water crisis **76**.22, 26-8
government and planned policies of **76**.8-9, 17
and multinational water corporations **76**.29-30
pricing mechanisms **76**.22, 32
and privatisation **76**.22-3, 32
and wars over the ownership of water resources **76**.22
water meters **76**.36, 38
water pollution **76**.1, 5, 10-11; **146**.36
causes of **76**.4, 7, 8, 9
in the developed world **76**.10-11
in developing countries **76**.4, 10
and global water supplies **76**.10-11, 15
and multinational water corporations **76**.29-30
statistics **76**.9

and water shortages **76**.36
water stress, calculating **76**.15-16, 17
water supplies **76**.15-17
financing the provision of **76**.31-2
and food production **76**.3, 4, 7, 18
and multinational water corporations **76**.29-30
and planned water management policies **76**.8-9, 17
projected worldwide water use **76**.35
statistics **76**.1, 2, 4, 6, 8, 19, 20
and water as a human right **76**.24-5, 32
and water pollution **76**.10-11, 15; **146**.36
and water shortages **76**.15-17, 19, 21-2; **146**.13
water usage by sector **76**.3
and water users **76**.36
water vapour emissions, aircraft **119**.16
watershed, television **121**.37
erosion of **121**.38-9
wave power **97**.2, 6, 12
wealth
children's perceptions of **149**.9-12
inequality **149**.19, 22, 27
and segregation **115**.32
weapons and violent crime **137**.7-8
weapons testing, animal experiments in **103**.1
weather patterns and climate change **97**.1
Web 2.0 **158**.6
webmail **158**.3
websites
and bullying **122**.20, 21
and suicide **136**.37-9
terrorist **147**.8-9
wedding costs **134**.25
weddings rings, history of **106**.20
weight *see* body weight; obesity
weight loss
drug treatment **162**.2-3, 6, 20
and exercise **162**.20, 36
financial incentives **162**.22-3
and lifestyle changes **162**.20
surgery **162**.3
weight monitoring in schools **127**.36; **162**.16
weight problems *see* obesity; underweight people

Volume numbers appear first (in bold) followed by page numbers; a change in volume number is preceded by a semi-colon.

Vol. **74** Money Matters
Vol. **76** The Water Crisis
Vol. **78** Threatened Species
Vol. **81** Alternative Therapies
Vol. **82** Protecting our Privacy
Vol. **85** The Housing Crisis
Vol. **88** Food and Nutrition
Vol. **89** Refugees
Vol. **96** Preventing Sexual Diseases
Vol. **97** Energy Matters
Vol. **99** Exploited Children
Vol. **100** Stress and Anxiety
Vol. **103** Animal Rights
Vol. **106** Trends in Marriage
Vol. **107** Work Issues
Vol. **115** Racial Discrimination
Vol. **116** Grief and Loss
Vol. **117** Self-Esteem and Body Image
Vol. **118** Focus on Sport
Vol. **119** Transport Trends
Vol. **120** The Human Rights Issue
Vol. **121** The Censorship Debate

Vol. **122** Bullying
Vol. **123** Young People and Health
Vol. **124** Parenting Issues
Vol. **125** Understanding Depression
Vol. **126** The Abortion Debate
Vol. **127** Eating Disorders
Vol. **128** The Cannabis Issue
Vol. **129** Gambling Trends
Vol. **130** Homelessness
Vol. **131** Citizenship and National Identity
Vol. **132** Child Abuse
Vol. **133** Teen Pregnancy and Lone Parents
Vol. **134** Customers and Consumerism
Vol. **135** Coping with Disability
Vol. **136** Self-Harm
Vol. **137** Crime and Anti-Social Behaviour
Vol. **138** A Genetically Modified Future?
Vol. **139** The Education Problem
Vol. **140** Vegetarian and Vegan Diets
Vol. **141** Mental Health
Vol. **142** Media Issues
Vol. **143** Problem Drinking

Vol. **144** The Cloning Debate
Vol. **145** Smoking Trends
Vol. **146** Sustainability and Environment
Vol. **147** The Terrorism Problem
Vol. **148** Religious Beliefs
Vol. **149** A Classless Society?
Vol. **150** Migration and Population
Vol. **151** Climate Change
Vol. **152** Euthanasia and the Right to Die
Vol. **153** Sexual Orientation and Society
Vol. **154** The Gender Gap
Vol. **155** Domestic Abuse
Vol. **156** Travel and Tourism
Vol. **157** The Problem of Globalisation
Vol. **158** The Internet Revolution
Vol. **159** An Ageing Population
Vol. **160** Poverty and Exclusion
Vol. **161** Waste Issues
Vol. **162** Staying Fit
Vol. **163** Drugs in the UK

welfare reform bill **135**.23
welfare support *see* state benefits
whales
    hunting **78**.6, 13, 14
    watching **78**.13-14
wheelchairs **135**.7
wholegrain foods **88**.15
WiFi hijacking **158**.37
wild animals
    in animal experiments **103**.6
    as food **140**.17
    and the fur trade **103**.38-9
wildflowers, threatened species in Britain **78**.36
wildlife
    captive breeding **78**.22
    conservation **88**.32, 34; **146**.33
        and the exotic pet trade **78**.21-2
    crime **78**.19, 38-9
    illegal souvenirs **156**.32
    illegal trade in **78**.21-2
    killing of **78**.2, 4-5, 5-6
    and the law **78**.16-17, 38-9
    in London **85**.16-17
    and new house-building in the south-east **85**.33
    overcollecting **78**.22
    rare species **78**.28
    trade **146**.34
        live animals **78**.20-1
    vulnerable species **78**.28
    and water abstraction **76**.34, 36
wills **74**.16
    and lone parents **133**.38
wind energy **97**.2, 4, 5, 6, 9, 21, 38
    and climate change **97**.15
    costs of **97**.16
    energy available from **97**.5
    new wind farm projects **97**.5
    and noise **97**.17
    numbers of wind farms **97**.11
    offshore **97**.12, 16, 26
    opposition to wind farms **97**.12
    public attitudes to **97**.16
    top myths about **97**.15-17
    turbines **97**.5, 15, 17, 38
    in the UK **97**.13, 26
Windows 7 **158**.22-3
wine
    consumption, young people **123**.1
    health benefits **143**.4
    strength **143**.1
winter deaths, older people **159**.4
wireless networks **158**.5
withdrawal symptoms
    cannabis **128**.15
    gambling **129**.30
    nicotine **145**.26-7
withdrawing or withholding treatment **152**.3, 5-6
witnessing bullying **122**.1-2
women
    and abortion
        decision-making **126**.16

        rights **126**.21
        views on abortion time limit **126**.36, 37-8
    and ageing population **159**.5
    and alcohol
        and heart attack risk **143**.7
        pregnant women **143**.3, 25, 27, 33-4
    and body image *see* body image, women
    disabled, violence against **135**.27
    and divorce **106**.26, 31
    employment prospects **107**.32
    equality and child labour **99**.12
    and fertility *see* fertility; infertility
    and the future of work **107**.12
    and gambling **129**.21, 34
        online gambling **129**.27
    gender pay gap **107**.13, 25, 26; **154**.2-3, 6, 30, 35-9
    glass cliff/glass ceiling **107**.9; **154**.34, 38
    and globalisation **157**.4
    graduate salaries **139**.36
    and HIV/AIDS **96**.20, 24-5, 29, 30-1
    and homelessness **130**.15
    Internet usage **158**.4
    low self-esteem **136**.2
    maternity leave **107**.16, 21
    and mental ill-health **141**.1
    and migration **150**.2, 15
    and online shopping **134**.16
    and part-time working **107**.17
    post-natal depression **125**.4, 17-18
    and poverty **160**.15, 25
    pregnant women **88**.7
    and prison **137**.39
    and sexually transmitted infections (STIs) **96**.3, 9
    single **106**.3, 20
    and smoking **145**.21, 22
    social mobility **149**.21
    sperm creation **144**.29
    in sport **118**.18-20, 21-2
    and stress **100**.13
        frequent worrying **100**.19
    and suicide **136**.33, 35
    violence against **137**.8
    working mothers **107**.26
women in the workforce **149**.21; **154**.29-34
    equal pay *see* gender pay gap
    European Union **154**.33
    glass ceiling **107**.9; **154**.38
    glass cliff **107**.9; **154**.34
    in the media **154**.11
    non-traditional careers **154**.31-2
    in senior positions **154**.17, 29, 34
wood, recycling **161**.25
woodland
    burial grounds **116**.39
    planting on landfill sites **161**.33
words to describe racial identity **115**.4-5
work
    effects of cannabis use **128**.14
    exploitation of workers **120**.28-31
    gambling at work **129**.22-4
    and mobile phones **158**.13

past retirement age **159**.10, 15
work experience and specialist diplomas **139**.24, 25
work and gender *see* gender and work
work-from home scams **134**.27
work intensity, EU **154**.18
work-life balance **107**.6, 14, 16; **154**.30
Work Permit System **150**.23
work-rich and work-poor families **149**.28
Workability project **135**.15
workaholism **107**.29
Worker Registration Scheme (WRS) **150**.6
working abroad **107**.3
working class **149**.3
   attitudes to money **149**.19-20
   attitudes to moving home **149**.26
working conditions
   garment industry **157**.27-9
   international companies **157**.11
   migrants **150**.19, 20
working hours *see* hours of work
working mothers **107**.26; **154**.29
working parents **107**.21-2, 24-5, 26
   effect on families **124**.1, 21
   role of father **124**.7-8, 11
working poor **160**.5
Working Tax Credit **133**.35
workophiles **107**.2
workplace
   age discrimination **159**.8-13
   and disabled people **135**.15
   dismissals
      reasons for **82**.28
      unfair **82**.26, 27
   drug testing **128**.20
   exercise **162**.23, 24
   gambling **129**.22-4
   gender gap **154**.17-18
   obesity discrimination **162**.21
   and privacy rights **82**.25-30
      and CCTV **82**.26, 27
      company policies on electronic communications **82**.30
      European-level regulation of **82**.28

   personal information **82**.30
   racism **115**.11-14
   smoking ban **145**.14
   surveillance **120**.32-3
   travel plans **119**.32-3
workplace bullying **122**.27-39
   anti-bullying policies **122**.39
   avoiding **122**.35
   defining **122**.27, 28, 37
   effects **122**.30, 31, 33, 37-8
   and harassment **122**.30
   responses to **122**.27, 31-2, 33, 37-8
   signs **122**.27, 28-9, 37, 39
   and small businesses **122**.36
   support **122**.31-2, 38
World Anti-Doping Agency (WADA) **118**.25, 27
World Anti-Doping Code **118**.27, 31-2
World Bank **157**.8, 10, 17
World Cup, effect on mental health **141**.23
world food supply, and GM crops **138**.9, 10, 34-5
World Fit for Children, A **120**.3
World Fit for Us, A children's forum **120**.3
World Summit for Children **120**.3
world trade *see* international trade
World Trade Organisation (WTO) **88**.33; **157**.2-3, 8, 13-14, 17, 21-4
   and global water supplies **76**.5, 23
   and the liberalisation of water **76**.29
World Wide Web (WWW) **158**.2-3
worries, young people **123**.2-3
worship **148**.1

Y

yoga **81**.3, 30, 39
   and back pain **162**.33-4
   and exam stress **100**.5
young children
   gender differences in achievements **154**.23
young offenders
   custody **137**.12, 15, 19

Volume numbers appear first (in bold) followed by page numbers; a change in volume number is preceded by a semi-colon.

Vol. **74** Money Matters
Vol. **76** The Water Crisis
Vol. **78** Threatened Species
Vol. **81** Alternative Therapies
Vol. **82** Protecting our Privacy
Vol. **85** The Housing Crisis
Vol. **88** Food and Nutrition
Vol. **89** Refugees
Vol. **96** Preventing Sexual Diseases
Vol. **97** Energy Matters
Vol. **99** Exploited Children
Vol. **100** Stress and Anxiety
Vol. **103** Animal Rights
Vol. **106** Trends in Marriage
Vol. **107** Work Issues
Vol. **115** Racial Discrimination
Vol. **116** Grief and Loss
Vol. **117** Self-Esteem and Body Image
Vol. **118** Focus on Sport
Vol. **119** Transport Trends
Vol. **120** The Human Rights Issue
Vol. **121** The Censorship Debate

Vol. **122** Bullying
Vol. **123** Young People and Health
Vol. **124** Parenting Issues
Vol. **125** Understanding Depression
Vol. **126** The Abortion Debate
Vol. **127** Eating Disorders
Vol. **128** The Cannabis Issue
Vol. **129** Gambling Trends
Vol. **130** Homelessness
Vol. **131** Citizenship and National Identity
Vol. **132** Child Abuse
Vol. **133** Teen Pregnancy and Lone Parents
Vol. **134** Customers and Consumerism
Vol. **135** Coping with Disability
Vol. **136** Self-Harm
Vol. **137** Crime and Anti-Social Behaviour
Vol. **138** A Genetically Modified Future?
Vol. **139** The Education Problem
Vol. **140** Vegetarian and Vegan Diets
Vol. **141** Mental Health
Vol. **142** Media Issues
Vol. **143** Problem Drinking

Vol. **144** The Cloning Debate
Vol. **145** Smoking Trends
Vol. **146** Sustainability and Environment
Vol. **147** The Terrorism Problem
Vol. **148** Religious Beliefs
Vol. **149** A Classless Society?
Vol. **150** Migration and Population
Vol. **151** Climate Change
Vol. **152** Euthanasia and the Right to Die
Vol. **153** Sexual Orientation and Society
Vol. **154** The Gender Gap
Vol. **155** Domestic Abuse
Vol. **156** Travel and Tourism
Vol. **157** The Problem of Globalisation
Vol. **158** The Internet Revolution
Vol. **159** An Ageing Population
Vol. **160** Poverty and Exclusion
Vol. **161** Waste Issues
Vol. **162** Staying Fit
Vol. **163** Drugs in the UK

risk factors 137.13, 14, 16-17
and street homelessness 130.11
types of crime 137.11-12, 16
young parents and non-traditional families 124.20-21
young people
 and abortion 126.13, 17-18, 28-9
  confidentiality 126.13, 28, 29
  telling parents 126.28, 29
  views on abortion for disability 126.35
 affordable housing for 85.3-4
 and age discrimination 159.12
 attitudes to biotechnology 138.16
 attitudes to marriage 106.5
 attitudes to mental ill-health 141.25
 bereavement support 116.28
 and cannabis 163.9, 30
  behavioural effects 128.16
  possession 128.27
  cannabis use 128.6, 21
  education about risks 128.28
  penalties for use 128.9
 as carers 135.10-12
 and child pornography 132.30
 and citizenship see young people and citizenship
 and contraception 123.22; 126.23
 and crime see young offenders; youth crime
 and criminal justice system 137.17, 19
 and debt 134.24
 and depression 123.27-8; 125.8, 9
 and divorce 124.29-30, 34
 and domestic abuse 155.21, 26
 and drug abuse 123.14; 163.3, 9, 15-16, 18-19; 26-30
 and eating disorders 123.33-4
 and emotional problems 123.10
 fear of 137.26-7
 and funerals 116.23
 and gambling 129.1
  gambling addiction 129.25, 31, 32-3
  National Lottery 129.11-13
  signs of problem gambling 129.38
  views on gambling 129.13
 and gender violence 155.21
 and grief 116.19-28
 health-related behaviour 123.1-3
 and healthy eating 88.4
 and HIV/AIDS 96.17, 24-9, 38
 homelessness see homeless young people
 house prices and first-time buyers 85.6, 7
 and identity (ID) cards, opposition to 82.7
 and the Internet 158.27
  online gaming addiction 158.39
  online risks 158.28
 and justice system 120.1-2, 12-13
 media habits 142.38
 media representation 142.15
 and mental health 123.9; 125.16
 and mental illness 141.25
 and money matters 74.1-4, 14-17
  attitudes to money 74.2
  budgeting 74.2, 3, 14-15, 23
  credit cards 74.15, 16

  debt 74.1, 2, 15, 16, 23-4
  and insurance 74.2, 15
  paying bills 74.2
  pension planning 74.1-2; 159.21
  savings 74.15
  teenagers 74.8-9
Muslims
 and fundamentalist beliefs 147.16-17
 help to reject extremism 147.34
 and multi-faith environments 148.32-3
 negative representation of 137.24, 25
 news awareness 142.32
 and nutrition 123.1, 6-7
 and obesity 123.31
 parenthood see teenage parents
 parenting teenage children 124.16-17
 and the police 137.14
 and politics see young people and citizenship
 poverty and mental illness 141.22
 and pregnancy see teenage pregnancies
 and religion 148.34
 rights 120.1-22
 and safety 137.20
 and self-harm 123.36-9; 136.2, 4-19
 and sex 123.19-21
 as sex abusers 132.29, 30
 and sex education development 133.15-16
 sexual exploitation of teenagers 99.20-2
 and sexually transmitted infections (STIs) 96.3, 4, 8-9, 25; 123.25-6; 133.2-3, 12-13, 17
 as single parents 126.31
 and smoking 123.11-13; 145.1, 2-6
  influence of films 145.9-10
  nicotine patches 145.20
 and social exclusion 149.38-9
 and sport 118.2
 and suicide 123.35; 136.27-8
 teenage girls
  body image 117.20-21
  and domestic violence 155.26
  eating habits 117.20
  plastic surgery 117.26-8
 unemployment 149.38-9
 as victims of crime 137.13, 17
 voting rights 120.7-8
 and world trade 157.17
young people and alcohol 123.1-2, 9, 14-19
 alcohol misuse 143.29, 37
 alcohol consumption 143.2, 5, 15, 20, 37
 drinking habits 123.1-2, 19; 143.2, 5, 15-17, 21, 37
 eating problems 127.20-21
 effects of 123.15
 exceeding daily benchmarks 143.8
 getting help 123.14
 and HIV 96.26
 influence of others 143.17
 influence of television soaps 143.18-19
 and the law 123.16; 143.2, 17
 obtaining alcohol 143.16, 17, 20, 28
 problems 123.18-19
 proposals to cut underage drinking 143.5, 29

risks **123**.14
safety information **123**.16, 17
statistics **123**.1-2
under-age purchase of alcohol **143**.16, 20, 28
young people and citizenship **131**.26-39
civic involvement **131**.31-2
and decision-making **131**.28
and the EU **131**.39
feelings of exclusion **131**.26
involvement in politics **131**.35
and mock elections **131**.27
political interest **131**.28, 31, 32, 35
political party support **131**.32
views on citizenship **131**.31-2
youth councils **131**.33-4
youth parliaments **131**.29, 33-4
Young People into 2006 report **123**.1-3
Young People's Parliament (Birmingham) **131**.34
Young Scot **131**.34
youth detention centres, restraint techniques **120**.17
youth councils **131**.33-4
youth crime **137**.11-27
causes **137**.13, 14
costs **149**.39
and education **137**.13
extent of **137**.11, 14, 16
gender differences **154**.25
and mental health **137**.13
statistics **137**.11, 16
types of offence **137**.11-12, 16
and victimization **137**.13
youth custody **137**.12, 15, 19
Youth Inclusion Programmes (YIPs) **137**.12
Youth Inclusion and Support Panels (YISPs) **137**.12
youth justice **120**.12, 13
statistics **137**.19
Youth Justice Board **137**.12
Youth Offending Teams (YOT) **137**.12
and ASBOs **137**.23
youth parliaments **131**.29, 33-4
youth unemployment, costs of **149**.38-9
youth work

and extremism prevention **148**.30-31
interfaith **148**.33
single-sex **154**.5
YouTube **142**.35; **158**.21-2

Z

Zen Buddhism, and Kinhin (walking meditation) **100**.10
Zen macrobiotic diet **140**.2
zero carbon eco-towns **151**.32
zero-emission fuels **151**.28-9
zero waste initiatives **161**.7, 34
zinc **88**.6; **140**.3-4
zoo conservation **78**.24-50

Volume numbers appear first (in bold) followed by page numbers; a change in volume number is preceded by a semi-colon.

Vol. **74** Money Matters
Vol. **76** The Water Crisis
Vol. **78** Threatened Species
Vol. **81** Alternative Therapies
Vol. **82** Protecting our Privacy
Vol. **85** The Housing Crisis
Vol. **88** Food and Nutrition
Vol. **89** Refugees
Vol. **96** Preventing Sexual Diseases
Vol. **97** Energy Matters
Vol. **99** Exploited Children
Vol. **100** Stress and Anxiety
Vol. **103** Animal Rights
Vol. **106** Trends in Marriage
Vol. **107** Work Issues
Vol. **115** Racial Discrimination
Vol. **116** Grief and Loss
Vol. **117** Self-Esteem and Body Image
Vol. **118** Focus on Sport
Vol. **119** Transport Trends
Vol. **120** The Human Rights Issue
Vol. **121** The Censorship Debate

Vol. **122** Bullying
Vol. **123** Young People and Health
Vol. **124** Parenting Issues
Vol. **125** Understanding Depression
Vol. **126** The Abortion Debate
Vol. **127** Eating Disorders
Vol. **128** The Cannabis Issue
Vol. **129** Gambling Trends
Vol. **130** Homelessness
Vol. **131** Citizenship and National Identity
Vol. **132** Child Abuse
Vol. **133** Teen Pregnancy and Lone Parents
Vol. **134** Customers and Consumerism
Vol. **135** Coping with Disability
Vol. **136** Self-Harm
Vol. **137** Crime and Anti-Social Behaviour
Vol. **138** A Genetically Modified Future?
Vol. **139** The Education Problem
Vol. **140** Vegetarian and Vegan Diets
Vol. **141** Mental Health
Vol. **142** Media Issues
Vol. **143** Problem Drinking

Vol. **144** The Cloning Debate
Vol. **145** Smoking Trends
Vol. **146** Sustainability and Environment
Vol. **147** The Terrorism Problem
Vol. **148** Religious Beliefs
Vol. **149** A Classless Society?
Vol. **150** Migration and Population
Vol. **151** Climate Change
Vol. **152** Euthanasia and the Right to Die
Vol. **153** Sexual Orientation and Society
Vol. **154** The Gender Gap
Vol. **155** Domestic Abuse
Vol. **156** Travel and Tourism
Vol. **157** The Problem of Globalisation
Vol. **158** The Internet Revolution
Vol. **159** An Ageing Population
Vol. **160** Poverty and Exclusion
Vol. **161** Waste Issues
Vol. **162** Staying Fit
Vol. **163** Drugs in the UK